BATTLESTAR
GALACTICA™
VAULT

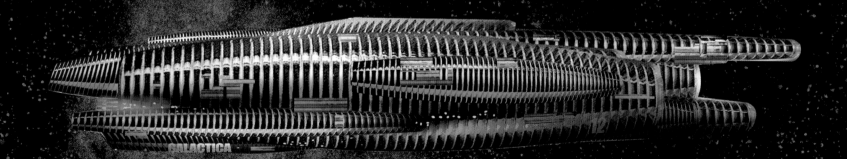

BATTLESTAR GALACTICA™ VAULT

By Paul Ruditis

Aurum
Press

TITLE PAGE: Concept art by Ralph McQuarrie, showing an explosive encounter between a Battlestar's cannons and Cylon Raiders attempting an attack.

CONTENTS

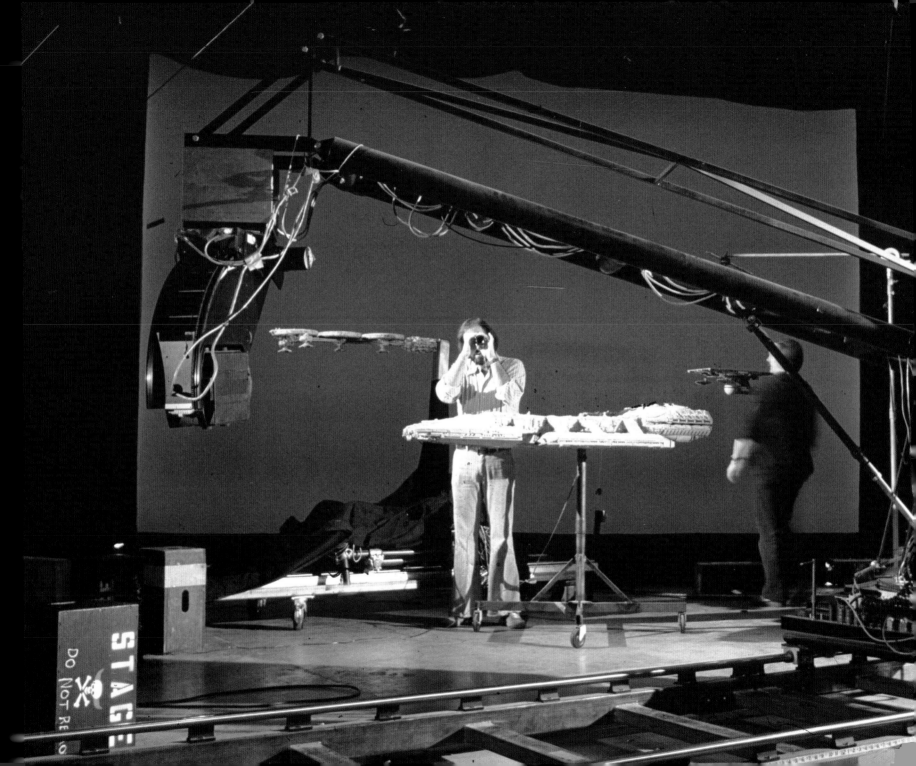

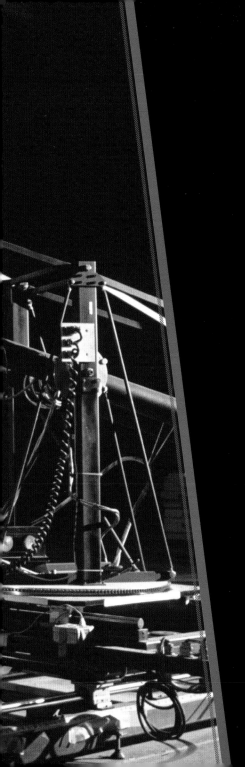

INTRODUCTION

WHEN I WAS SIX, I WANTED TO LIVE ON A SPACESHIP and have a robotic

pet dog. I wanted to be Boxey from my favorite TV show, *Battlestar Galactica*. The idea of

living an adventure every day, stowing away to a frozen planet or being trapped in a burn-

ing inferno, terrified me in the exciting way that dreams sometimes do. It was so much more

interesting than my daily life going to school or riding my green machine up and down the

driveway. And, let's be honest, I already had the bowl haircut. But those dreams of intergalac-

tic adventure didn't end there …

At eleven, I wanted to be friends with the Ewoks and live in the trees.

By fourteen, I longed to be Wesley Crusher piloting a starship, facing down a Klingon threat

on the viewscreen in front of me.

The seventies and eighties were a great time to be a child who dreamed of adventure

among the stars. Science fiction was in the midst of a sort of golden age in family adventure,

taking whiz-bang action series in the vein of Flash Gordon and Buck Rogers and repurposing

them for all audiences, introducing new, young viewers to long-established tropes.

LEFT: Visual effects crew setting up a shot with the *Galactica* (center), a livery ship (upper left), and a flat-top-style ship (middle right) for the original *Battlestar Galactica*. The effects would be shot with a "Dykstraflex" camera system (foreground).

Many of these shows worked on two levels, blending kid-friendly entertainment with more thought-provoking adult themes. Certainly a lot of the references in *Battlestar Galactica* went over my head. At six years old, I couldn't imagine what a "socialator" was, to say nothing of the philosophical explorations of the Beings of Light and their freedom of choice. But I did love how the Vipers flew through space taking out the Cylon Raiders.

Battlestar Galactica was groundbreaking television in the seventies no matter what critics at the time may have said. While the TV show may not have been able to compare to what was happening in movies, with their seemingly inexhaustible budgets, the special effects and epic scope of a civilization on the verge of extinction was unprecedented in weekly television. This was both its blessing and its curse. The promise of *Battlestar Galactica* had a difficult time keeping up with the production realities of the era, no matter how advanced the special effects were.

As I grew up, popular science fiction experienced its own growing pains along with me. Genre television became darker and more complex, expanding beyond straight science fiction and delving into horror and fantasy as well. Shows like *The X-Files* or *Buffy the Vampire Slayer* achieved more critical respect … except when the latter series introduced its adorable kid sister character.

By the new millennium, the stories I clung to in my youth matched my maturity. Audiences rebelled against kid-friendly additions to serious drama. Or perhaps they always had. As an adult, I can look back and understand why grown-ups might not have thought the cuteness level of the Ewoks compensated for their surprising ability to take down the most powerful force in the galaxy. Occasionally, I too began to wish that Wesley would shut up.

I'm glad to say that I never completely lost my appreciation for the childlike innocence in some science-fiction shows, but at the same time, I have been able to appreciate the more mature dramas. By the time the new version of *Battlestar Galactica* aired in 2003, that series had reached a new maturity as well.

The reimagined *Battlestar Galactica* was equally as groundbreaking in special effects as the original had been in its time. But the new series and its spin-off *Caprica* aired during a period in which great changes were happening across the television landscape beyond technical achievements. Storylines were becoming darker, with antiheroes and straight-up villains becoming the protagonists. Serialized storytelling was replacing episodic structure as shows grew more epic in scope. New avenues for viewing shows were being developed in different media formats.

In many ways, the shows that shared the name *Battlestar Galactica* were alike in their approach to space adventure and mythology. In other ways, there was a vast universe of difference between them. Both had devout audiences and could evoke passionate debate. There was a social aspect to the shows that traditional dramas and comedies did not usually depict. And each had a message for the viewers to decipher on their own and to debate with other fans.

The *Battlestar Galactica* of my adulthood may have been different from the one of my youth, but I enjoyed them both for how they fit with my life at the time. I refuse to pick a favorite because I consider them two sides of the same coin, working together to form a whole in a franchise that spans most of my life.

Though I may never forgive the producers of the reimagined *Galactica* for getting rid of Boxey so quickly.

1 | BUILDING A UNIVERSE

A GROUP OF THE MOST PROMINENT PEOPLE ON EARTH—scientists, astronauts, politicians, sports figures—gather in a strange building in the Nevada desert for a mysterious event. They are all experts in their respective fields, the best that society has to offer, brought together for some vague reason that is not remotely the true purpose of this conclave. As they meet to discuss "important things," the ground suddenly rumbles. Someone—an actress, a journalist—looks out the window to see that this strange building has detached itself from the ground and lifted off like a rocket, making its way to the stars. These select people are Earth's last hope for the continuation of the human race on the eve of the planet's destruction. They have been sent out, wandering the heavens in search of a new home.

Such was the premise behind *Adam's Ark*, a science-fiction television show concept that Glen A. Larson came up with long before the creation of *Battlestar Galactica*. Unfortunately, the then-fledgling writer had this idea in the late sixties at roughly the same time *Star Trek* was being considered a failure for NBC. Television networks were hesitant to risk their budgets on another "space opera" as the genre was soon to be called, especially on a writer who had yet to establish himself.

LEFT: One of the earliest images of the *Galactica* and the Colonial ragtag fleet appeared in the art created by conceptual designer and illustrator Ralph McQuarrie. The Colonials would have many adventures in space, interacting with species on other planets, fleeing the Cylons, and trying to find allies as they sought out a shining planet known as Earth.

The idea was placed in a drawer, but not entirely forgotten while Larson built his name writing and producing procedural dramas, mysteries, and action adventures. The science-fiction story came back years later in a different form when a seismic shift occurred in Hollywood, making stories set among the stars something less risky. This time, the ark had become a fleet and the humans were not *from* Earth, but traveling in search of that shining planet. Fans have called into question the authenticity of Larson's story of *Adam's Ark* over the years, but there is no doubt that a certain science-fiction film franchise awakened interest in the genre in the late 1970s.

There is no way to discuss the original *Battlestar Galactica* without mentioning *Star Wars*. The two are inextricably tied, though both by coincidence and design. The success of the film for 20th Century Fox and George Lucas had a major impact on Hollywood in 1977, and suddenly everyone was in the science-fiction business. On screens big and small, aliens were *in* and rip-roaring space adventure was all the rage. Paramount Pictures brought back *Star Trek* in motion picture form and Universal Pictures was looking for a franchise of their own to mine for the small screen.

Universal executives tapped one of their now go-to producers, Glen A. Larson. Larson had come a long way from his early days as a writer and was entering the boom time of his career. During the late seventies, a half-dozen TV series were produced under his shingle. Shows like *Quincy M.E.*, *The Hardy Boys / Nancy Drew Mysteries*, and *B.J. and the Bear* were being churned out on a weekly basis by his stable of writers and production personnel. Larson specialized in commercially popular series that families could sit down and watch together, offering a little something for everyone. They weren't necessarily critical darlings, but they had mass appeal.

Larson had previously produced two of the *Six Million Dollar Man* TV-movies, but those stories about a man with bionic body parts were the producer's only experience in the science-fiction genre up to that point. Later, Larson would mine sci-fi and fantasy elements in future shows like his television adaption of the pulp serial character, *Buck Rogers in the 25th Century,* and the pop-culture phenomenon *Knight Rider*, but his specialty tended toward action shows and procedurals set on present-day Earth. None of his series—not even *Buck Rogers*—would compare to the epic space adventure of *Battlestar Galactica*.

Although Larson's exposure to science fiction was limited at the time, he worked with supervising producer Leslie Stevens for the pilots of both *Battlestar Galactica* and *Buck Rogers*. An experienced science-fiction television writer from his time as executive producer on *The Outer Limits*, Stevens had teamed up with Larson on other shows. Stevens's contributions to the *Battlestar Galactica* pilot movie "Saga of a Star World" were likely valuable, but his work did not carry over to the series that followed.

RIGHT: Space was a new frontier for Glen A. Larson, but his experience with *Battlestar Galactica* led the way for his next series, *Buck Rogers in the 25th Century.*

A BATTLE AMONG THE STARS

Battlestar Galactica was packed with action from the start—along with the allusions to ancient mythology that the show would become known for. Like the ruse of the Trojan Horse, a gift from the Greeks to the city of Troy, the Cylons use the false promise of peace to hide an explosive ambush leading to the near annihilation of the Twelve Colonies of Man. The surviving Colonials are sent fleeing in a caravan of ships led by the lone remaining battlestar named *Galactica*, chased by the rarely seen Cylons and their robotic Centurion soldiers. This innovative idea took place decades before dystopian stories became popular in the mass market and helped lay the groundwork for a genre that would be all the rage decades later.

In an interview with the Archive of American Television in 2009, Larson recalled that the series went through roughly 200 names, with numerous people at the studio contributing to the process. The overriding edict was that Universal wanted the word "star" in the title. Seeing how this convoy was being led by a spaceship, or *star*ship, that was basically a futuristic battleship, the term *Battlestar* was born. Original terms like *battlestar*, the measurement of time known as a *yahren*, and the expletive *frack* were part of the many unique facets of this alien society.

Battlestar Galactica drew heavily on historical inspiration—most notably Moses fleeing Egypt with the Israelites—but it didn't end there. Larson's own Mormon faith was clearly an influence, with names like The Quorum of Twelve and the planet Kobol adapted from the scriptures of the Church of Jesus Christ of Latter Day Saints. Character names were taken directly from Earth's mythology and production design mirrored imagery seen throughout human history, particularly with Egyptian influences.

Tying these Colonials to humans set up a mystery for an audience that wanted to understand how this race that was so alien at times was also quite familiar. Why did the planet Kobol resemble Egypt?

LEFT: Ralph McQuarrie's concept for the bridge of *Galactica* was far grander than the final design, but elements like the computerized workstations and the seating on multiple levels carried through to the final set.

Who were these Lords of Kobol and what ties did they have to our own myths? The series may have had a clear goal in finding Earth, but it was these parallels with our history that made it unique.

Unfortunately, before the pilot movie even aired, few people saw these original elements, instead focusing on the similarities to *Star Wars*. It was a comparison that *Battlestar Galactica* would face throughout its relatively brief life on television. Admittedly, some of that was by design.

Both *Battlestar Galactica* and *Star Wars* centered on an older mentor and two young, male heroes: one an idealistic youth, the other a bit of a rogue. Robotic Cylons replaced armored Stormtroopers. Viper spacecraft followed an aerodynamic design not unlike an X-wing starfighter. But more than themes, the two projects set in the stars shared people behind the scenes—most notably concept designer/illustrator Ralph McQuarrie and special effects artist John Dykstra.

PICTURED: Some people mistakenly remember the Centurions as the Cylons, but the actual race was reptilian in design and concept. The rarely seen Cylon Imperious Leader was often shown in shadow, but the sketch (this page) designed by Jean-Pierre Dorléac gives more insight into the character's look, which grew out of McQuarrie's concept art (opposite page, lower right).

For *Battlestar Galactica*, McQuarrie would create designs for the Viper fighters and Cylon Raiders as well as for the *Galactica* itself. His work not only set out the physical specifications for the ships, but also set the tone for the project as a whole. His concepts were among the first pieces created during pre-production of the series. As with *Star Wars,* his designs helped sell the project. His artwork was even included with the scripts that went out to actors, giving them a hint of how the show they signed on to would evolve.

McQuarrie's conceptual artwork was often more impressionistic in design, but it laid out a vision for the series that inspired everything from set pieces to the development of the universe's mythology. A piece of art he created for "Saga of a Star World" would greatly influence the final promotional artwork for the launch of the series. That art piece, incorporating members of the cast, ships, Cylons, and even the daggit Muffit would become the most recognizable image associated with the series for decades to come, used on DVD and soundtrack covers, and various supplemental materials.

Although George Lucas came up with the idea for *Star Wars*, it was Ralph McQuarrie who, more than anyone else, is credited with developing the look of the movie. The concept artist drew the designs for many of the characters in the film, from Darth Vader to Chewbacca and the droids, as well as the ships, planets, and other visuals seen on screen. His early work on the project is believed to have been integral to selling 20th Century Fox on the original idea and to helping secure funding for the film.

ABOVE: Ralph McQuarrie's vision for *Battlestar Galactica* set the stage for the action-packed show that fans would grow to love.

GALACTICA

saga of a star world

GALACTICA

GALACTICA

saga of a star world

THIS PAGE: McQuarrie's conceptual artwork used to pitch the series evolved in stages, from a version featuring a Cylon Raider in pursuit of a Colonial Viper (bottom) to a draft highlighting the insectoid Ovions (top). These and other versions ultimately served as a template (left) for the final promotional art that would be associated with the show for decades to come.

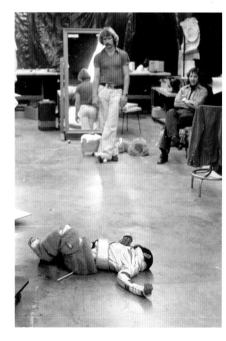

John Dykstra had just wrapped up work on *Star Wars* with George Lucas's Industrial Light and Magic—a company Dykstra helped form—when he joined the *Battlestar Galactica* team. The Academy Award®–winning special effects supervisor was at the forefront of special effects back when the craft was in its nascent days in Hollywood. Special effects weren't new to television in the late seventies, but the changes taking place in that field were dramatic, thanks largely to Dykstra's own work on *Star Wars*. The master technician had been instrumental in developing what he'd coined the "Dykstraflex" camera, a digital motion control camera system used for filming complex special effects shots. The new technology would come in handy for *Battlestar Galactica*, a series that was to be filmed on a weekly schedule.

Certainly, an undertaking of this magnitude had never been attempted before on television. Even *Star Trek*'s duel-style battles with two ships facing each other while suspended in space were mild compared to the promised action of *Galactica*'s Viper squadron taking on the Cylon

PICTURED: The visual effects team was involved in building many props and costumes for *Battlestar Galactica*, including that of the Muffit suit based on Ralph Massey's concept model. The chimps, Evie and Doc, spent a great deal of time at the special effects studio with handler Boone Narr. The goal was to get the chimps as accustomed to the suit as possible prior to filming.

Raiders. The effects were so integral to the series that the visual effects team began their work on the pilot episode "Saga of a Star World" months before the actors were even cast and almost a year before the pilot aired on ABC.

By today's standards, the special effects would appear almost quaint, but they were cutting-edge at the time, a fact that *TV Guide* reporter Bill O'Hallaren was almost giddy about in his cover story on the launch of the series. For the article, Dykstra posed with the ship central to the show, his 72-inch model of the *Galactica*. O'Hallaren compared the youthful crew's impressive slate of spaceship models to playing with toys.

Today, visual effects on television are created with computers, but back then they were more physical in design. Ship models were designed and built in a painstaking process so they would look real on-screen. Dozens of models were built for the series and stored at Dykstra's special effects house where they were used in massive space battles filmed in miniature scale.

Largely due to the special effects work, Universal set a budget of roughly one million dollars per episode, making it the highest priced television show in history at the time. Studio executives likely assumed that the investment was more than justified seeing as how *Star Wars* had already grossed about a quarter of a billion dollars in its first year and a half of release. The "Saga of a Star World" TV-movie that would launch the series was unprecedented in spending, shooting for more than fifty days when the schedule had

ABOVE: Only one Viper mockup, constructed of a metal skeleton, plywood and removable wings for easy transport from location to location, was built for filming the original series.

FIGHTER-BOMBER

FIGHTER-BOMBER

THIS PAGE: Additional concept art by Andrew Probert for "Saga of a Star World" expanded upon his designs for the Viper fighters. The larger bombers were intended to fly with the Vipers but went unused. Here, special effects designer Grant McCune and special effects supervisor Richard Edlund work with Viper models.

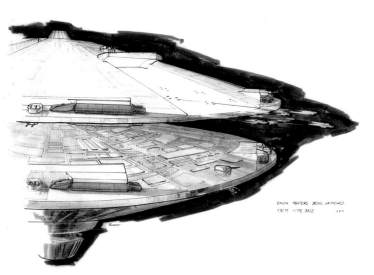

originally called for only twenty-seven. The money would be seen

on-screen through models, space scenes, and action unlike anything

ever experienced outside of movie theaters.

To avoid any conflicts between the two *Star* properties, producers and

lawyers for *Battlestar Galactica* and *Star Wars* came together to hash out

a set of rules to keep the two universes distinct from one another. The

producers on *Battlestar Galactica* agreed to a list of parameters to avoid

infringing on the unique look of the *Star Wars* universe. According to Larson, one such rule established that the *Galactica* team would not develop

guns that fired laser beams. Instead, the special effects crew created laser pistols that relied largely on sound effects and a flash from the muzzle

to show a shot had been fired, which likely helped save on effects shots.

(Later episodes of the series did feature red laser pulses firing from the

weapons.) The agreement would not be enough to head off a lawsuit.

THIS PAGE: Basestar concept art by Andrew Probert and its visual effects
model, made from a plexiglass and acrylic frame, in the process of being built.

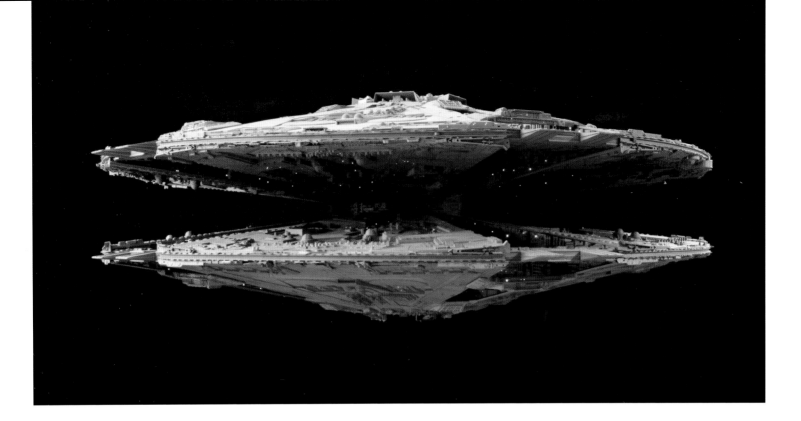

Hoping to forestall the release of "Saga of a Star World," 20th Century Fox filed suit for copyright infringement and unfair competition and trade practices. The judge set the case for spring, thus ensuring the series would get its premiere, but the time spent on depositions and preliminary court battles would impact production of the TV series. Universal countered the suit by filing an action

of their own, claiming that *Star Wars* had infringed on their earlier film *Silent Running*. The original lawsuit citing *Galactica*'s copyright infringement was ultimately decided in 1980 in Universal's favor, though it was later overturned on appeal. By that time, it was almost a pointless endeavor as the series had already been cancelled twice.

ABOVE: The original Basestar visual effects model from the collection of Gary Cannavo. Fiber optics were run through the model castings to give the impression of light flowing through the ship's windows and other openings.

"Battlestar: Galactica"

JEAN-PIERRE DORLEAC
·78·

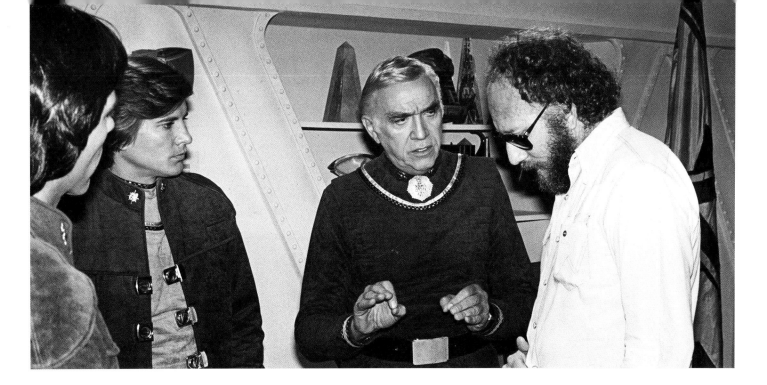

LIFE IN THE STARS

The faces that would grace the screen in *Battlestar Galactica* were as important as the special effects, if not more so. Leading this ragtag fleet was Lorne Greene as Commander Adama. Best known for his patriarchal role on *Bonanza*, the second longest running Western series on television, Greene was already well-known in family-oriented television. This was important in establishing that *Battlestar* was a part of the family-hour brand of entertainment ABC wanted for the series. Unfortunately, that same family-hour mentality would later work against the show, but Greene's fatherly presence both on-screen and off bonded the cast and their characters.

For the heroic Apollo, son to Adama, ABC wanted a young actor named Richard Hatch. At first, the actor was reluctant to join a science-fiction series in spite of the fact that he grew up loving the

---

OPPOSITE PAGE, CLOCKWISE FROM LEFT: Jean-Pierre Dorléac's designs for Colonial-wear included these sketches illustrated by Haleen Holt for the cold weather uniform seen extensively in "Gun on Ice Planet Zero" as well as the traditional warrior uniforms.

THIS PAGE: Actors Richard Hatch and Dirk Benedict listen in as Lorne Greene talks with director David Bellisario.

genre itself. Hatch feared the baggage that was believed to come with such roles. He eventually came around and accepted the part that became the moral center of the show, his character often clashing with his father and others when they started down a darker path. Hatch had spent two years on ABC's popular soap opera *All My Children* before going on to guest spots in multiple shows and taking over as one of the lead actors in *The Streets of San Francisco* after Michael Douglas left. Glen Larson was largely unfamiliar with the actor's work, but he and Univer-

sal agreed to the casting. It was an important sign of unity because there was a fight brewing with the other male lead in the series.

Apollo's counterpart, Starbuck, was designed to be a bit of a rogue. The pyramid-playing, cigar-chomping ladies' man didn't operate by the same moral playbook as Apollo and Adama, but his loyalties were true, and he ultimately did what was right … no matter what path got him there. Glen Larson and Universal Studios executive Charles Engel met with a young actor named Dirk Benedict in New York at the Sherry-Netherland Hotel in the fall of 1977. According to Benedict's autobiography, *Confessions of a Kamikaze Cowboy*, that was the moment he'd landed the role … at least, as far as the producer and studio were concerned.

The theater-trained actor hadn't had many notable parts on television at that point. In fact, he'd even taken some time off from acting. But Larson had recalled Benedict's previous work and brought him in for the meeting. During the informal get-together, Larson, Engel, and

LEFT: The sons of Adama: Apollo (Richard Hatch) and Zac (Rick Springfield).

even Engel's wife bonded immediately with Benedict. The meeting came early enough in the development process that Larson reportedly molded the role of Starbuck around the actor. In their eyes, he was Starbuck. Unfortunately, ABC did not agree.

The network engaged in months of back-and-forth with Larson and the studio over the casting of Starbuck, bringing in several alternate choices, including Don Johnson. Benedict was forced to perform screen test after screen test, jumping through the network's hoops to prove that he was right for the role. Every note the network came up with—saying he couldn't handle the drama, the romance, that he wasn't sexy enough—was answered by another screen test.

It went on for months. So long that when production for "Saga of a Star World" began on March 3, 1978—in front of a soundstage packed with media covering the event—one of the key players, Dirk Benedict, was nowhere to be found. The role of Starbuck was still not filled. As Benedict recalled in his autobiography, it took a private

RIGHT: Director David Bellisario and actor Richard Hatch between takes of *Battlestar Galactica*.

THIS PAGE: The Cylon Centurions under Baltar's (John Colicos) lead were the primary villains of the lone season of *Battlestar Galactica*. They continue their chase of the fleet from the first episode through to the last when Commander Adama decides to turn the tables on the Cylons and go on the offensive in "The Hand of God" with a surprise attack on a Basestar.

At right, Ralph McQuarrie concept art depicting Baltar inside a Cylon Raider cockpit with two Cylon Centurions.

meeting between the network and studio executives in a Bel Air mansion to settle the matter. Benedict admits that he does not know what conversations took place during that tête-à-tête, but he started work on March 8.

The trio of Adama, Apollo, and Starbuck would be the backbone of the series, and a strong cast of actors—both familiar to audiences and relatively unknown—were there to support them. Second-in-command would be Colonel Tigh, played by Terry Carter, who had worked with Larson before on *McCloud*. Herbert Jefferson Jr. and Tony Swartz would star as colonial warriors Boomer and Jolly. Laurette Sprang was hired as Cassiopeia, who began her role as a "socialator" before quickly moving into medicine as a medtech and Starbuck's primary love interest.

Maren Jensen, a largely unknown actress, was hired to play Adama's daughter, Athena, another love interest for Starbuck and the third part of the show's main love triangle. Rick Springfield rounded out

Adama's family, playing Apollo's ill-fated brother, Zac. Springfield, of course, would go on to fame in the ABC network soap opera, *General Hospital*, before launching the singing career that would make him a household name.

Another short-lived role went to Jane Seymour, who played Serina, a reporter who would be sealed in marriage to Apollo before meeting her untimely death in "Lost Planet of the Gods, Part 2." To entice younger viewers, Noah Hathaway was cast as Serina's soon-to-be orphaned child, Boxey. The actor, who would later go on to star in another cult favorite, *The Neverending Story*, became best known for his relationship with his robotic daggit—a Colonial version of a dog—Muffit. John Colicos, a veteran television actor with numerous guest and starring credits to his name, played the primary villain in the series, Baltar. Later in the series, Anne Lockhart would join the cast in the role of Sheba, a Viper pilot from another battlestar.

JOURNEY'S END?

Universal launched *Battlestar Galactica* with an almost unprecedented press blitz for "Saga of a Star World," with major articles in *Time, People*, and *TV Guide*. When *Newsweek* ran a cover story in their September 11, 1978 "fall season preview" issue featuring the unheard-of *Battlestar Galactica,* they did so with the headline "Son of Star Wars" in big, bold letters. "TV's 'Battlestar Galactica'" was written below in a notably smaller font.

To help generate publicity for the new series—and hopefully recoup some of the production cost—a theatrical version of "Saga of a Star World" was released in movie theaters in select global markets months before the episode aired in the United States. This version of the film had several differences from the television episode, the most notable change being that the Cylons' Imperious Leader orders the death of Baltar by beheading in the original version. When that ending did not test well with audiences, it was reshot to have Baltar survive and become the primary villain in the series.

In spite of—or *because* of—the comparisons to *Star Wars*, viewers turned out in large numbers to watch "Saga of a Star World" when it premiered on ABC on September 17, 1978. Complicating the broadcast was the fact that it was interrupted for nearly an hour on the east coast with the network breaking news coverage of the signing of the Israel-Egypt peace accord. It was a fitting tie-in to the series that mirrored the ancient Israelites' flight from Egypt, but not exactly helpful in enticing an audience to enjoy the TV-movie. But the viewers stuck around to see the end of the more than three-hour event and eventually came back for more.

As the season evolved into weekly hour-long episodes, the demanding schedule took its toll on production. Scripts were notoriously late, pushing back the special effects work and music scoring. Hours were long with the actors spending more of their day on-set and in

their trailers than in their homes. John Dykstra and most of his special effects team left after four episodes, turning over the effects work to Universal's new Hartland Visual Effects unit. This change further exacerbated the scheduling problems. To cut time and cost, the special effects team often reused shots, leading to space battles that looked familiar as the same ships followed the same paths to destruction.

In spite of its problems, *Battlestar Galactica* continued to chug along. The ratings dropped throughout the season, but the series still managed to attract viewers and special guests. Lloyd Bridges came onboard for the significant role of Commander Cain, in charge of the *Battlestar Pegasus*, another surviving ship of the fleet. Other notable guest stars included Ray Bolger, Bobby Van, and even Fred Astaire, who Larson claims

ABOVE: Universal's unprecedented media blitz resulted in several magazine cover stories for the series, like the one that headlined *TV Guide's* issue released during the launch of the fall television season. The advertising campaign relied heavily on Ralph McQuarrie's concept art as seen in the two-page ad for the series.

FOREARM WEAPON — FIRED
THROUGH DIRECT NERVE IMPULSE
OR MUSCULAR MOVEMENT.

took on the role largely because his grandchildren loved the show.

Critics were not as enamored with the series. Reviews tore apart the production, comparing it to *Star Wars* every chance they got, seemingly ignoring the fact that television and film were dramatically different mediums and the expectations should be different. It became known as "escapist" television viewing, suggesting that it was somehow a lesser experience than more high-minded dramas. Certainly, some criticism of the series was warranted, but many dismissed the genre of science fiction altogether—an opinion that persists to this day, considering the lack of attention the genre generally receives at Emmy® time.

Years later, in his interview for the Archive of American Television, Glen Larson admitted that it would have been better for the series to follow the track of his other hit show, *Quincy, M.E.* The forensic procedural began its life as part of the *NBC Mystery Movie* franchise produced by Universal Studios. It was part of a rotating series of two-hour mystery television movies before becoming a weekly show in its own right. If *Battlestar Galactica* could have followed that path—which had been the original plan—it would have allowed the show time to build its audience and the production to craft stronger scripts and create unique special effects.

The family-hour time slot was also considered a detriment to the show, Fred Astaire's grandchildren notwithstanding. Placing the series on Sunday nights at eight o'clock curtailed some of the action, lessening the drama. While it was largely permissible for humans to kill the robotic Cylons, the network censors were squeamish about human casualties. This dramatically weakened the threat of the villainous Cylons, who many fans complained simply couldn't shoot straight because they rarely hit their targets.

When CBS moved the very popular *All in the Family* into the eight o'clock time slot, the scheduling shift chipped away at the *Battlestar Galactica* ratings even further. Spending a million dollars per episode made a bit less sense when the series fell out of the top ten, and then

LEFT: The Cylon Centurion costumes were created from the sketches of concept designer Andrew Probert, who envisioned the beings as reptilian in appearance. Ralph McQuarrie had suggested the artist for what became his first Hollywood job before going on to work on other notable franchises like *Star Trek* and *Back to the Future.*

later slipped from the top twenty. ABC was the number one network in the country with over half of the top ten series in the Nielsen ratings, including the hugely popular Garry Marshall sitcoms *Laverne & Shirley, Happy Days,* and *Mork & Mindy.* By the end of the 1978–79 season, *Battlestar Galactica* was cancelled with *Mork & Mindy* set to replace it in the Sunday night family-hour in the fall.

"The Hand of God" was the last episode of *Battlestar Galactica* to air on ABC that year. In it, the crew of the *Galactica* receives their first real hint that Earth indeed did exist via a subspace recording from the planet. Though the series only lasted a season, it won the People's Choice Award for "Favorite New TV Dramatic Program." It was also nominated for a number of critical and industry awards, receiving Golden Globe® nominations for "Best TV Series, Drama" and a nomination for "Best TV Actor, Drama," for Richard Hatch. In addition to a nomination for "Outstanding Art Direction in a TV Series" at the Emmy® awards, the series went on to win for "Outstanding Costume Design for a Series" for "The Man with Nine Lives" and "Outstanding Individual Achievement—Creative Technical Crafts" for the special effects in "Saga of a Star World."

Battlestar Galactica may have been gone from the airwaves, but it would live on in other ways. Props and sets were recycled for use in Larson's other science-fiction series, *Buck Rogers in the 25th Century*, but that little piece of *Galactica* wasn't enough for the fans. A letter-writing campaign, supported by Larson and the production team, began in the hopes of bringing back the series, much like how *Star Trek* managed its own resurrection. Producers had already been planning for the second season, looking for ways to expand the story and possibly even dismiss the toothless Cylon threat for good. Among the changes behind the scenes, they were hoping to augment the writing staff with someone with actual science-fiction experience: Isaac Asimov, who had initially been a critic of the series.

On ABC the following fall, *Mork & Mindy* dropped precipitously in the ratings when it took over the eight o'clock Sunday night time slot. This suggested to some that *Battlestar Galactica*'s challenges might not have been the fault of the production company. After some time and thought, ABC decided to give the show another chance and bring it back as a series that would eventually become known as *Galactica 1980*. Having already seen the series struggle in the ratings, the network was not ready to commit to the same price tag as before, insisting that Larson make changes to streamline the production.

For a variety of reasons, most of the cast did not return. To explain the different crew, Larson set the new series thirty years in the future with an adult Boxey now serving under the seemingly un-aged Lorne Greene as Adama and Herbert Jefferson as Colonel Boomer.

The central conceit behind the new *Galactica* was that the fleet had finally found Earth. The new heroes, Troy (Kent McCord) and Dillon

RIGHT: Promotional photo from "The Man With Nine Lives" of Richard Hatch and Dirk Benedict posing with special guest Fred Astaire. The acclaimed dancer and actor played Chameleon, a Colonial con man posing as Starbuck's father.

(Barry Van Dyke) brought a group of Colonial children to the planet in an attempt to integrate into society and help protect their cousins from the Cylon threat. The more Earth-based setting would help save on costs, but the new slimmed-down budget made itself evident on-screen in story, effects, and pretty much every aspect of the show. *Galactica 1980* lasted only ten episodes before going out with a whimper, which led most fans, and even Glen Larson himself, to agree that the series best be forgotten.

But the original *Battlestar Galactica* would not be so easily dismissed. The lone season of *Battlestar Galactica* generated only twenty-four episodes, which is barely a quarter of the number required to secure a

ABOVE: A Cylon extra chatting with young fans during a break in the filming. The actors often removed their helmets immediately after their scenes were shot as they were notoriously hot and difficult to see through.

traditional syndication deal promising reruns of the show in perpetuity. At the time, television shows existed almost entirely for syndication deals. That was where the studios made their real money, selling the repeat episodes to air off-network. This was years before video and DVD sets added another source of revenue, to say nothing of online streaming. Without additional outlets to air, *Battlestar Galactica* could have easily faded into obscurity, if not for the small but vocal fanbase and the hard work of a number of people associated both directly and indirectly with the series.

Universal did manage to recoup some of their investment by putting the series back in cinemas internationally with *Mission Galactica: The Cylon Attack*, combining the re-edited episodes of "The Living Legend" and "Fire in Space." A later film was also built from recut episodes of *Galactica 1980*, but it was in printed form that the original series would continue for years to come. Marvel Comics' monthly *Battlestar Galactica* comic line ran until 1981, and

Berkley Books' novels kept the series active with new stories running up until 1987. The same year, another momentous shift occurred with science fiction on television when *Star Trek: The Next Generation* premiered.

ABOVE: From the collection of Gary Cannavo, an original miniature of a bike, made of wood with model-kit tires and working lights to simulate rocket jets, was used on-screen during the filming of *Galactica 1980*. The rider is a toy doll with a hand-carved foam helmet.

1

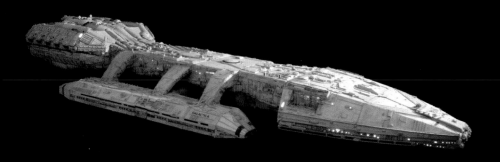

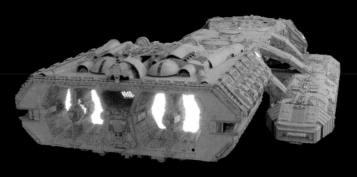

2

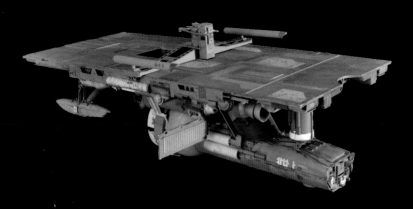

3

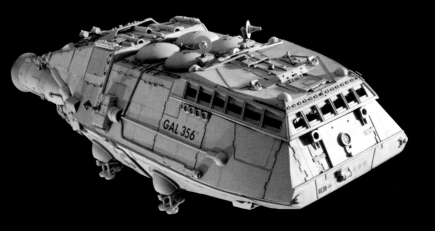

4

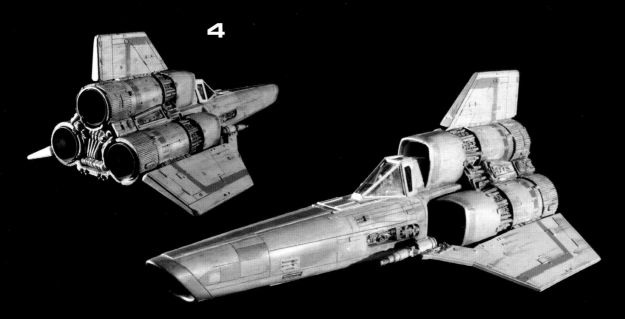

THE FLEET

1. *BATTLESTAR GALACTICA*
2. FLATTOP
3. *GALACTICA SHUTTLE*
4. VIPER
5. LIVERY
6. COLONIAL MOVERS
7. *GEMINI*

5

6

7

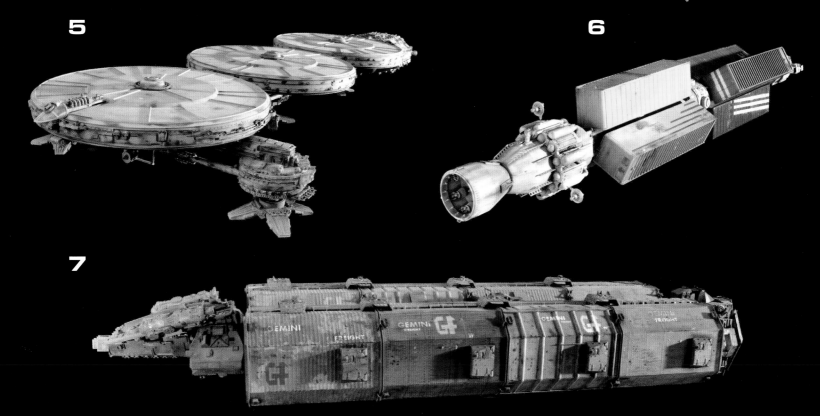

2 BATTLESTAR GALACTICA REIMAGINED

THE RESURRECTION OF *STAR TREK* FOR A NEW GENERATION was as important to the science-fiction community as the success of *Star Wars* a decade earlier. It brought new interest in the genre on television, proving that—even airing off-network in syndication—a science-fiction series could be a success. The show also gave a young writer by the name of Ronald D. Moore his first job in television, which would ultimately prove integral to the return of *Battlestar Galactica*.

Years had passed since Berkley Books published the last original *Battlestar Galactica* story, but the love for the series never waned among its core group of fans. In 2001, Studios USA, a division of Universal Television, tapped *X-Men* executive producer Tom DeSanto and director Bryan Singer for the first real shot at bringing the *Galactica* back to Earth. The production team obtained Glen Larson's blessing for the project and the creator came onboard as a creative consultant. The crew started pre-production in Vancouver, but unfortunate issues of timing and reports of creative conflicts led to the series ultimately being abandoned.

LEFT: The artwork hanging in Adama's office, depicting the First Cylon War. In the series, the piece was credited to the Colonial artist Montclair, but it was actually the work of additional art director Ken Rabehl. The prop team distressed the original to give it a weathered look before it was hung on set.

Another member of the original *Battlestar Galactica* team interested in its revival was Richard Hatch. The Apollo actor had been a guest at science-fiction conventions over the years and saw firsthand how much the series still meant to its fans. He proposed his own follow-up series to the original, building his case through a series of novels he coauthored and even a short pitch presentation he filmed incorporating new scenes for a potential series, though the idea never gained traction at the studio.

Universal next tapped David Eick, an established producer for popular genre shows to usher a new *Galactica* project into development. Eick turned to Ronald D. Moore, the aforementioned writer of *Star Trek: The Next Generation* and *Deep Space Nine*, to script the project.

Moore had been a fan of the original series as a child, remembering the famed *TV Guide* cover that announced the fall season in 1978. Since he hadn't seen the show in many years, the first thing he did was rent "Saga of a Star World" to get reacquainted with the series.

*NOTE: POOL SCULPTURE
AS POLISHED STEEL.

ABOVE: Ken Rabehl's concept sketch for the Riverwalk section of Caprica City, where several key scenes and flashbacks would occur in the series.

"What struck me the most was the resonance between the apocalyptic attack on the colonies and the fact that I was watching this just a couple months after 9/11," he recalls. "I realized this had a powerful resonance to the time and place that I was in. That's what spoke to me the most."

Moore understood that what was considered escapist entertainment in the seventies did not have the same draw in the post-9/11 era. The terrorist attack on the World Trade Center in 2001 not only impacted production on the DeSanto/Singer version of *Battlestar Galactica* that failed to materialize, it continued to color the universe Moore and Eick were creating. In their desire to produce a series more grounded in reality than in science fiction, they had to take a darker approach to the concept of a civilization that had fled to prevent the very extinction of its race.

Moore saw other possibilities in the series, not the least of which being that it spoke to his own interests. "I liked the aircraft carrier metaphor of it," he says. "It was different enough from *Star Wars* in that it was literally a carrier in space. *Star Wars* is not. Even though they have fighter pilots and fighters and all of that nomenclature, they don't really play them like carrier battle groups and that sort of thing. So it felt distinct."

A large part of the reason Moore appreciated the naval analogy of the series was that he was already a fan of aquatic explorations of the new frontier. He'd previously integrated his passion into *Star Trek: Generations*, cowritten with Brannon Braga, by setting early scenes in the film on the sailing ship *Enterprise*. "My production company's

LEFT: Series executive producers David Eick (left) and Ronald D. Moore (right) with line producer Harvey Frand (center) who passed away in 2009.

called Tall Ship Productions," he explains. "I have this long love affair with naval history and ships and crews and combat crews and how ships are organized, all that. I knew that I could really bring up that aspect of the show and really make it much more strongly an aircraft carrier/battleship in space."

The man who brought Moore on in the first place took a different approach to the series. David Eick largely disregarded the source material in an effort to bring a fresh take to the project when it came across his desk. "This may come off as heresy, but I never really considered the original *Battlestar Galactica* one way or the other," Eick says. "I'm not contemptuous of the original show at all, I respect it as my show's ancestor and I understand the impulse to compare and contrast the two series, but I'm always a little upended when I'm asked that question—it's bizarre to think there was something called *Battlestar Galactica* before mine; like learning that someone used to live in your house with the same name as yours."

Eick freely admits that when he was originally approached by Universal to develop a reboot of the title, he was indifferent to the idea. "Beyond the crisp, catchy value of its basic logline, what I remembered of the old show—which I may have caught once or twice as a kid—was a somewhat campy echo of *Star Wars* and that was about it. I never went back and watched it before hiring a writer, never studied it once we got rolling along into serious development. It just wasn't relevant to what I wanted to do." That said, Eick was intrigued by the idea of the reboot for a couple of reasons. One of them had something to do with his competitive nature and his future producing partner's past work.

In the mid-nineties, Eick was the head of Sam Raimi's production company, developing first-run syndication television shows such as *Hercules: The Legendary Journeys* and *Xena: Warrior Princess*. These two shows in particular were a crowning achievement for him as they were the first dramas to beat *Star Trek: The Next Generation* in the syndication ratings. "As we were fierce competitors with that show, it

SPACE LINER, ONE OF THE
"BACKGROUND TRANSPORTS"

FEB 1 1 2003

FRONT VIEW

[SPACE LINER]

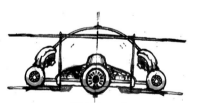

REAR VIEW

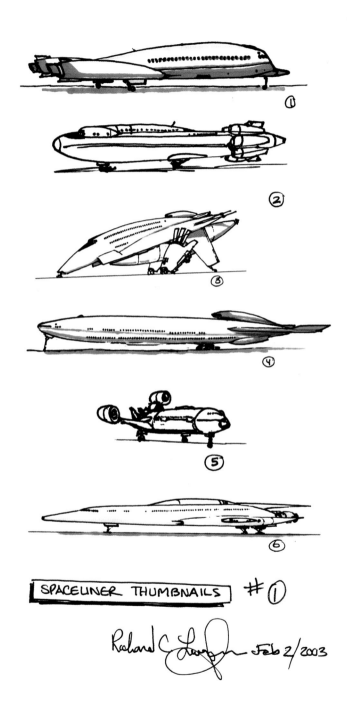

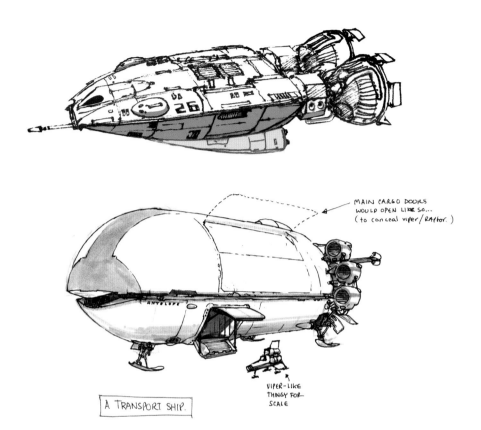

MAIN CARGO DOORS WOULD OPEN LIKE SO...
(to conceal viper/Raptor.)

A TRANSPORT SHIP.

VIPER-LIKE THINGY FOR SCALE

SPACELINER THUMBNAILS #①

Richard C Livingston Feb 2/2003

OPPOSITE PAGE, TOP: The Colonial Fleet mixed a little of the old and new as visual effects supervisor Gary Hutzel explains: "In the center band of ships, everything except the ring ship was from the original series. In front are the transport and liner that we added as well as *Colonial One*. Those and the ring ship were new ships for the reimagined show. The ring ship was the one ship I had nothing to do with the design of ... It was something that David Eick found and really liked ... The two concepts in the back were additional ships, which you rarely see, that we created to fill in the background. They were never identified as a specific ship in the series."

OPPOSITE PAGE, BELOW; THIS PAGE: Designs for the new ragtag fleet were created in homage to those from the original show. Concept artist Richard Livingston was hired to develop these background ships for the reimagined series, along with his work on the look for *Colonial One*.

was a badge of honor we wore proudly," he proclaims. By the time he had his own production company in 2001, there was still a *Star Trek* series on the air, potentially giving him the opportunity to beat *Star Trek* once again. "I figured this time it could be done by producing the kind of irreverent, tradition-defying 'space opera' that would send Trekkies running for the hills. And so there was the potential for a kind of poetic career symmetry to that challenge."

Having just come off producing a failed pilot for the USA Network, Eick was glad to hear the siren song of his first love calling him back. The show he'd been working on was a "cop show dramedy" that

fell apart at the last minute. "This followed all those years at Raimi's company, where we'd struggled so hard to push the envelope in horror, sci-fi, and fantasy, to reinvent what was possible to accomplish under TV constraints," he explains. "I know it sounds absurd, but I felt like I'd veered from my ordained path, and the gods had punished me by not picking up my cop show. Now, here was a chance to redeem myself, to go back to 'genre' filmmaking and the edgy subversion its storytelling beckoned (which cop show dramedies did not). In short, I was chomping at the bit to return to the world of blowing people's minds."

ABOVE: The *Galactica* port hangar bay was first brought to three-dimensional form as a paper model (left). The final set construction (right) bore a very close resemblance to the model.

ABOVE: The hangar bay set originated from a concept sketch by Ken Rabehl.

THE PLAN

With Eick and Moore onboard, the plan was to develop a miniseries to air on Syfy that, if popular enough, could go to a full series. Unlike earlier concepts, Syfy wasn't looking for a sequel to the original series. They wanted a whole new story built off the concept, a *reimagining*. Though there had certainly been reimagined television properties before, the word was still relatively young in Hollywood and to the general public at large, but it was quickly adopted by some and rebelled against by others.

Many fans of the original series had little interest in a reimagining. They wanted the old crew back. If not the old crew, they at least wanted stories that continued the journey of the fleet with which they were already familiar. But the network was adamant. And the producers, who had experience with devoted fan bases, were also looking to mine new territory. They just wanted to do it in a logical way.

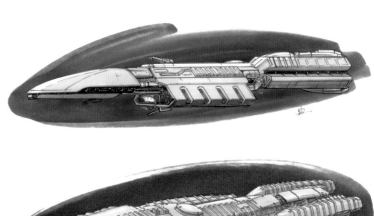

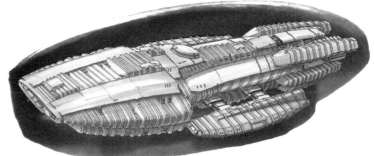

THIS PAGE: Concept designer Eric Chu came up with several options for the design of the *Galactica* which he drew up for the producers along with artists Chris Bell and Alex Leung. The top design was rejected for the *Galactica* but it was realized as another ship in the fleet for the *Razor* TV-movie.

OPPOSITE: Richard Livingston's sketches (bottom) for the *Galactica* were another important step in the development of the ship, seen in CGI rendering (top) after suffering heavy damage.

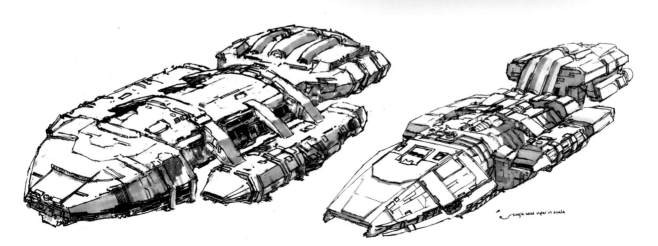

single seat viper in scale

THIS PAGE: Gary Hutzel: "We started out with a submarine shape [for *Galactica*] and then we added the ribbing to it in order to give it some more form to make it unique to the show. From the side, it did have a rounded shape. That's where it varies from the original series *Galactica*. It's much more rounded. Everything is curved as opposed to being squared off. There are lots of complex curves on it. So, consequently, if you put in the pods and you look at it from the side it looks kind of like a submarine. But everywhere else, it's very reminiscent of the original ship."

Richard C. Livingston
FEB 1
2003

THIS SPREAD: Richard Livingston's concept drawings for the *Galactica* not only proposed the general look of the ship, they also delved into the detail of the design for elements like the defensive battery rails and turrets that would be important for the many battle scenes in the series.

Visual effects supervisor Gary Hutzel's vision for the series matched what the producers were looking for, which he discovered in his very first meetings with David Eick and director Michael Rymer. Hutzel recalls: "In talking about it, I said, 'I think that we should do something different because Ron Moore's idea is so radically different than what has been done before. I think we should do away with lasers and phasers and we should have rocket engines on our spaceships. Not just glowing engines that push them along somehow magically.' That was a moment where everybody came together and said, 'That's exactly what we should do. When we fire a missile, you should have the missile trail behind. It shouldn't be just a phaser or photon torpedo or any of that kind of stuff.'"

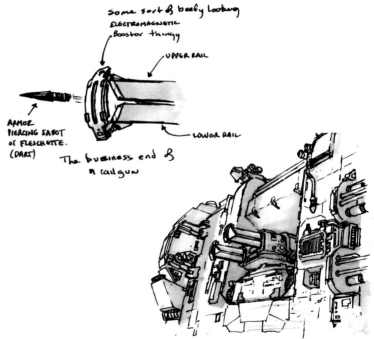

Some sort of beefy looking ELECTROMAGNETIC Booster thingy

UPPER RAIL

ARMOR PIERCING SABOT of FLESCHETTE. (DART)

LOWER RAIL

The business end of a railgun

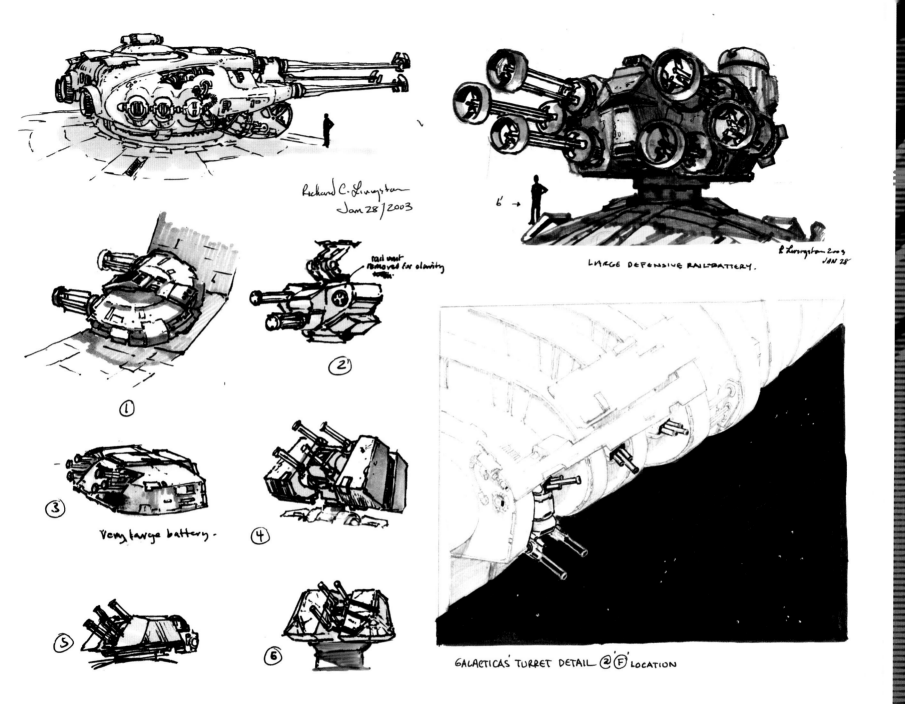

Richard C. Livingston
Jan 28 / 2003

LARGE DEFENSIVE RAIL-BATTERY.

R. Livingston 2003
Jan 28

6' →

rail mount
removed for clarity
here.

① ② ③

Very large battery.

④ ⑤ ⑥

GALACTICA'S TURRET DETAIL @ ② Ⓕ LOCATION

"One of the reasons I had the luxury of ignoring the original *Battlestar Galactica*," Eick explains, "was because by the time I'd settled on a writer for the project, Ron Moore, I knew *he* was going to study it. I figured if one half of the creative team was going to become an expert on the old show, it might actually be healthy for the other half to remain 'clean' of it—to maintain objectivity and to develop our story with no concern for its predecessor whatsoever. Also, Ron has a longer attention span than me. But I still firmly believe that decision—for us to be at once deeply conversant and yet blissfully ignorant of the original series—was a secret weapon key to our show's early success."

The reality was that the original *Battlestar Galactica* had aired twenty-five years earlier. Though the original series had a massive media campaign that had raised awareness at the time of its premiere, the ratings did drop steadily after the three-hour movie aired. The devoted fandom remained in love with the series for years,

PICTURED: From concept to execution, the design sketches laid out a plan the production team could follow for their exterior locations and interior set construction. Ken Rabehl's concept sketches (this page: Caprica City; opposite page: Baltar's lab) provided the foundation from which the look of the series was built.

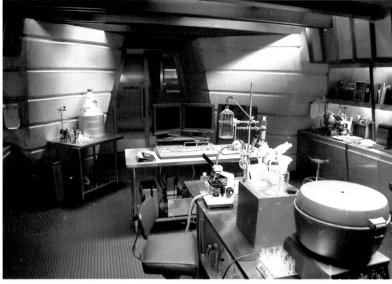

but the lack of available episodes on TV in syndication did not help grow that audience. Syfy successfully re-aired the original *Battlestar Galactica* decades later, but much of its audience was aware of the series in name only, having never seen an episode previously.

The option for developing a sequel series to a show about a fleet fleeing from an enemy would also suffer from the fact that it would potentially pick up late into the story. A continuation of the original *Battlestar Galactica* would effectively have to begin in the middle, long after the all-important attack of the Cylons. Approaching *Battlestar Galactica* as an entirely new series with throwbacks to the original would make it easier to attract new viewers, while hopefully not alienating fans of the 1978 series in the process.

"This sort of 'yin-yang' approach to the old series—paying homage in a few respects, ignoring it completely in others, and even going out of our way to subvert it in places—was quite deliberate," Eick admits. "We hoped that by maintaining a strident independence, such that

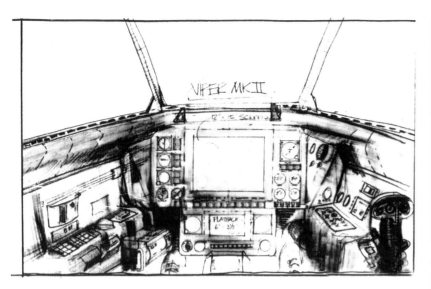

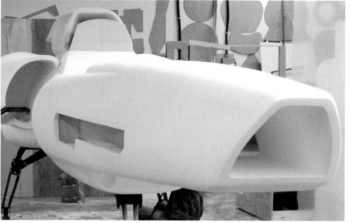

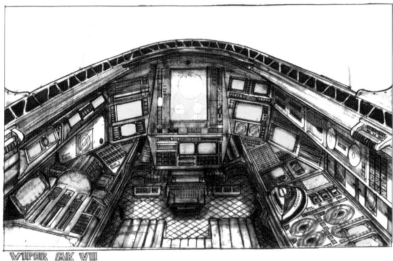

THIS PAGE: Technological differences between the Viper Mark II (top) and the Viper Mark VII (bottom) can easily be seen in the cockpit sketches for the two ships.

OPPOSITE PAGE: Eric Chu's designs for the Viper fighters would closely follow the model style seen in the original series, carrying over the airplane design as seen in this drawing by Chris Bell.

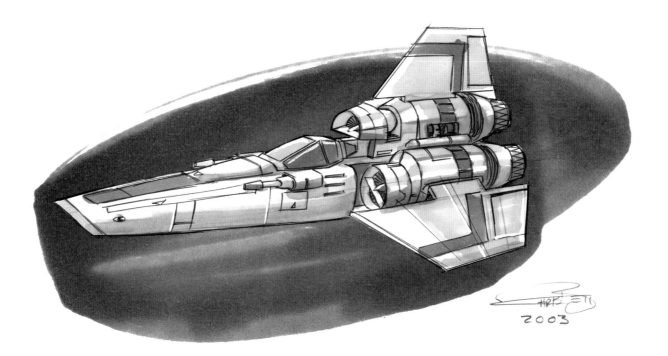

2003

our show would be palatable to someone who'd never even heard of the previous version—and then, incongruously, nodding and winking to a vintage detail in some overt way, to appease the faithful—we'd create a discordant vibe that would make it very difficult to pin our new show down or put it in a box. People would struggle to figure it out, and it would get under their skin. 'What the hell are they *doing*? Do they hate the old show or love it or *what*?!?' Exactly."

One decision that occurred early in the development process would be integral to the look and feel of the new series, establishing it as a very different product than the so-called escapist *Battlestar Galactica* of the seventies. The producers wanted to approach the filming almost as a documentary-style production, as if the story was real and the audience was viewing the characters through this lifelike lens. From a physical perspective, this meant often relying on

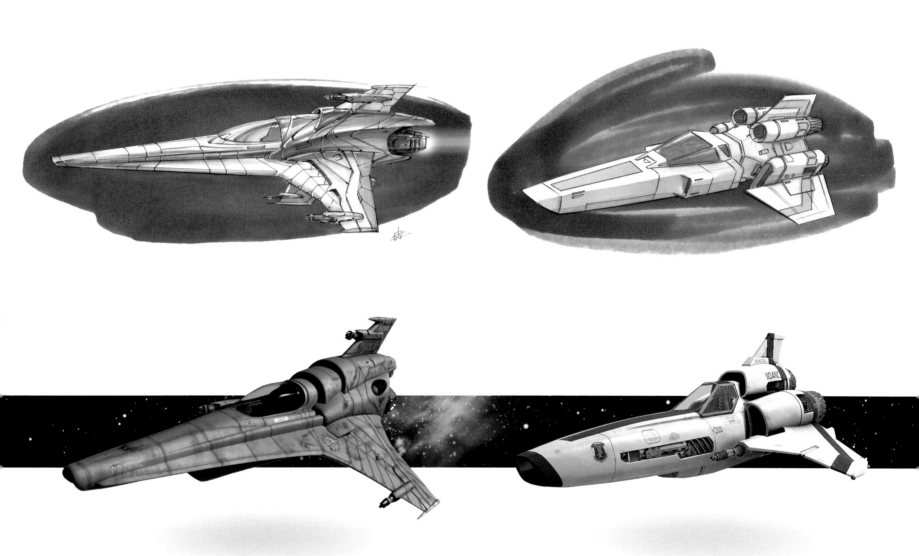

ABOVE: The Viper Mark VII and Mark II would appear as both physical models and CGI renderings. The final ships were built from the designs of Eric Chu, including the approved final concept art for the Mark VII (top left) and a preliminary sketch for the Mark II (top right) drawn by Chris Bell.

SC. 32

SC. 34A

SC. 36B

HOTDOG: "APOLLO, HOTDOG DEFENSIVE, THREE RIGHT FIVE AT TWO"

SC. 32A

SC. 36

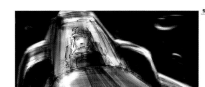

SC. 36C

LEE: " TALLY, HOTDOG, KAT, ON ME.

SC.34

SC.36A

SC. 36D

CAMERA PANS DOWN....

hand-held camera work to give the effect of a person with a camera mounted on the shoulder filming the action.

Director Michael Rymer, who had just come off the feature film *Queen of the Damned*, was brought aboard to establish a look for the miniseries and potential show to follow. The edict for a camera's-eye view of the action would be true for the smaller, more intimate scenes he directed on set as well as the CGI space battles that were developed in the visual effects house. Instead of the traditional perfect shots of beautiful ships in heroic battle, the goal was to present the action as if caught by someone looking out the window of another vessel. Ships might fly out of frame at times or not everything would be in focus, adding to the reality of the situation.

"It was a critical part of the franchise," Moore says of the decision to give the series a documentary-style viewpoint. "I think it was what grounded the show, what made the show different. And it gave it a sense of authenticity and truth to it. I sort of had this idea that, if

ABOVE: The visual effects team's digital storyboards helped directors envision the action that would be created in post-production. This was beneficial for shooting on set as they could direct the actors' reactions to what was taking place around them in space even though they were in an empty soundstage.

you're going to take the audience on a fantastical journey, you should root it in something. They should be rooted and grounded and they should believe as strongly as possible that these are real people who are about to go into this extraordinary occurrence."

This one directive colored the entire development of *Battlestar Galactica*. After years of working on a variety of *Star Trek* series, Moore wanted a different approach to presenting science fiction on television. "I love *Star Trek*," Moore is quick to note. "I can go on and on about how much *Star Trek* means to me, personally and to my career. However, there came a point where I was feeling like the style that show was in just felt stodgy and tired and it didn't feel real anymore. It just felt fake … Everything was smooth. Everything was perfect. It was just slow. It had no vibrancy to it, I felt, at a certain point. I wanted to mix it up and be edgier and be rougher and start to do more handheld stuff. I really wanted to break the form I felt I was kind of trapped in." His idea for a science-fiction series using handheld camerawork and docu-style filming was something he'd decided long before he had a science-fiction project to actually apply that style to. *Battlestar Galactica* would eventually give him the freedom to do just that.

Gone were the brightly polished sets and perfect uniforms that often graced the space opera. There would be no aliens of the week with bumpy foreheads learning a valuable lesson from the human

PICTURED: The visual effects team used green screen backdrops to extend the *Galactica* hangar deck beyond the confines of the soundstage. This practice would evolve to fully computer-generated backgrounds created for *Caprica*.

Gary Hutzel: "The [*Galactica*] hangar sets were only 1/50th the actual length of the hangar deck. We had a green screen at both ends so that we could show the extension, which is a hangar deck that ran something like eight hundred feet."

crew. Stories would not be neatly resolved at the end of an hour with a whole new adventure in another part of space the following week. "It was about stripping away a lot of things that I felt had become sci-fi artifice," Moore explains. "I wanted them to wear clothes that looked very normal. I wanted the technology to be accessible, phones with cords. I wanted the style of photography to convey this sense that these are real people and these are real events."

In laying out the physical look of the series, much of the work fell to the visual effects team brought in on the project, particularly the one led by Gary Hutzel of Zoic Sudios. Moore had worked with Hutzel before on *Star Trek: The Next Generation* and *Deep Space Nine*

and the effects house itself had been tangentially involved in the DeSanto/Singer version of *Battlestar Galactica* that failed to make it to the screen. With these experiences already under their belt, they went into the new series with a fresh approach on the visuals for the space opera. The days of model-making and practical special effects were over. The new *Galactica* would fly in a computer-generated universe with groundbreaking visuals matching the docu-style of camerawork through CGI design.

Production designer Richard Hudolin gave Gary Hutzel free rein on the look of the ships built on the computers of Zoic Studios. That freedom, however, did not extend outside of the production team.

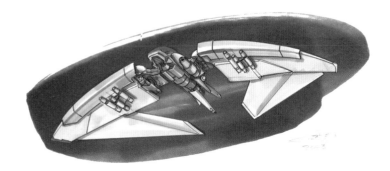

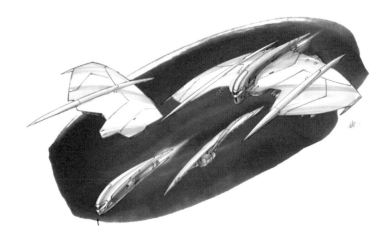

One of the larger issues early on in the pre-production phase was the design of the titular ship. The network wanted an entirely redesigned *Galactica* for their reimagined series. The producers knew that to keep fans—and themselves—happy, they had to stick as close to the original as possible. As Ron Moore explains, "I felt an obligation that if I was selling this as *Battlestar Galactica*, we were trading on that name and the history of that show, that it had to be *Battlestar Galactica* on some fundamental level." The producers and the network eventually settled on a compromise that took the same core design concept from the original, but gave it more of a modern submarine aesthetic.

Aside from the namesake battlestar, the Vipers kept mostly the same design and the other ships on the journey to Earth were built to mirror those in the original fleet. The Centurions would get a new, streamlined look, along with the Raiders. But the classic design of the Centurions was also built into the history of the show as early designs for the robot revealed that the initial models looked a lot like

LEFT: Early design concepts for the Cylon Raider went through many phases in trying to achieve the proper look for the ship. David Eick credits Studios USA executive Angela Mancuso with the breakthrough idea to turn the claw-like spires around so that they'd be at the front of the ships instead of the rear, which gave the Raiders the menacing quality they sought.

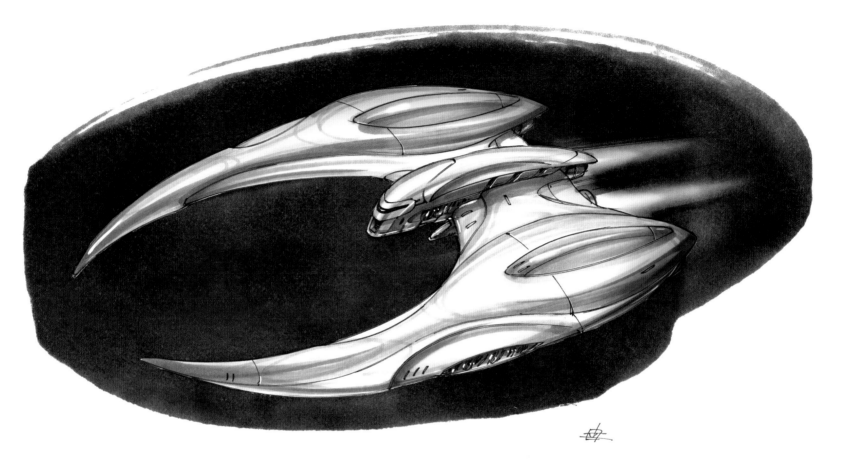

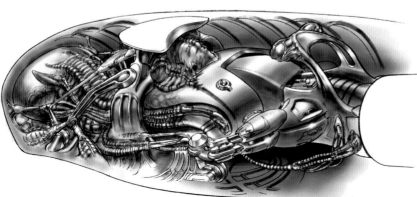

THIS PAGE: Eric Chu's final approved concept design for the Raider (top) shows the ship in its menacing glory while Ken Rabehl's concept art (bottom) reveals the most dramatic change to the reimagined design. Instead of being manned by a trio of Centurions as in the original series, the new ships would be bio-mechanical, combining organic and technological material.

THIS PAGE: The CGI model of the Cylon Basestar grew from the final design and detailed renderings that exchanged the original series' round spaceship models for the more star-like design.

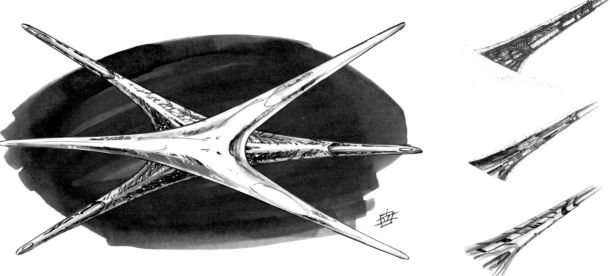

they had in the original series. In many ways, the reimagined series looked to the original in design and story, tying the two together while the writers forged their own path through the stars.

"My general approach was I wanted to keep everything that worked and discard everything that I felt didn't work," Moore says. "I wanted to have the basic superstructure in place with the family Adama, the aircraft carrier in space, the ragtag fleet, the twelve colonies, the Cylon attack. And then within that, 'Okay, what other elements can I bring back?' As we got into the series, then it became kind of fun. There were things to sort of touch on the old show—names, backstories, devices, frak—different little things that called it back … I never wanted to try to pretend that there was no lineage here, that there was no ancestor to our show. I always wanted to say there was that show first. We would not be doing this show if not for that show. I always wanted to honor that line, even as I was making changes." But it was those changes that all

RIGHT: The producers of the reimagined series could take the man out of the character, but they couldn't take the character out of the woman. Katee Sackhoff took on the gambling, hard-drinking, cigar-chomping role of Starbuck originated by Dirk Benedict and made it her own.

the fans of the original series would be talking about in the lead-up to the miniseries airing.

One of the first things producers caught flack for was one of the earliest decisions they'd made: changing Starbuck's gender. The production—and Starbuck's portrayer, Katee Sackhoff—would face the harshest criticism for that change long before the miniseries ever aired. Taking the beloved playboy of a character and making him female made little sense to the fans. Many dismissed the casting as an obvious way of pairing Starbuck with Apollo, played by Jamie Bamber. But more than just opening up romantic possibilities, the gender switch brought a host of new directions for the character—to say nothing about the fresh take on female roles in television, with the rules-flouting hotshot of a pilot being played by a woman.

Another controversial change came from the decision to make the newest models of Cylons human-looking. Rather than simply redesigning the Centurion models and making them better shots, this was a dramatic shift that did have roots in the original series. In the episode "War of the Gods," the *Galactica* crew runs into the seemingly omnipotent being, Count Iblis. At one point they posit the question of whether he could be an android built to look like a man. This concept would become reality in the reimagined series in a way that would conveniently save on production costs in not having to create as many CGI Centurions.

The mythology of the human-looking Cylons, or "skinjobs," and the exploration of their beliefs in comparison to those of the Colonials would become the backbone of the reimagined series. The decision also allowed the production to humanize the reimagined version of the duplicitous Baltar (James Callis) by giving him more three-dimensional Cylon characters to interact with. An ad campaign for the miniseries that focused on Tricia Helfer's Cylon, Six, made a bold statement that this was not your father's *Battlestar Galactica*.

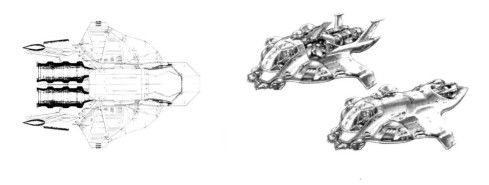

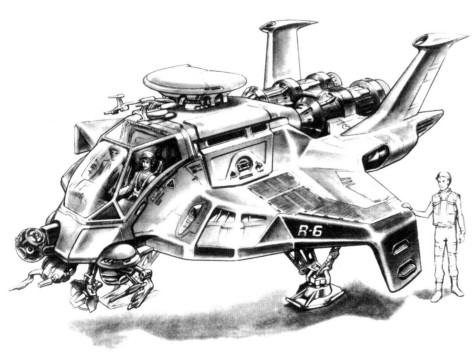

THIS PAGE: The Raptors that provided tactical support, scouting, and reconnaissance had no counterpart in the original series. These ships which began as Ken Rabehl's design sketches had both CGI versions and a foam and steel-frame model that could be lifted by crane for practical effects.

NEW LIFE AMONG
THE STARS

A benefit to *Battlestar Galactica* beginning its life as a miniseries was that it did not have to face the traditional casting process associated with a pilot for a television series. As David Eick explains, "One of the biggest hurdles you have to clear when producing a TV pilot is getting your cast approved. Unlike movies, in which an actor's approval is subject to the director and the studio (and maybe a co-star, if he/she wields that kind of power), TV is an infinitely more bureaucratic gauntlet of pain for the hopeful series regular. It's an arduous process you wouldn't wish on your worst enemy. And the hoop-jumping is endless: the casting directors, then the producers, then the studio execs, then the network—many of which, at any random point, can kill you."

Being a miniseries meant that the producers of the *Battlestar* pilot didn't have to demand a series hold option on most of the cast. If it had been a traditional hour-long pilot, the studio would have had to make deals with much of the large ensemble to ensure that they would be around if the series was picked up for an entire season. But going into the project as a miniseries meant most of the cast was hired for that one project, which meant the studio and network did not have to be so heavily involved in the casting. "This, as it turned out, was an unanticipated blessing," Eick recalls. "Because many of the supporting characters who would come to define the texture of *Battlestar* were handpicked in a little room in Vancouver by myself and director Michael Rymer—and that was that."

Edward James Olmos, Mary McDonnell, Jamie Bamber, Katee Sackhoff, James Callis, Grace Park, and Tricia Helfer were all considered "regulars" with series options, and therefore necessitated the standard approval process. "Some, like Eddie and Mary, were envisioned by Ron and me so early in the process that the roles were virtually written for them." Others, like Katee Sackhoff and Grace Park, had to audition multiple times. Of those two actresses in particular

Eick says, "They were neck-and-neck to play Starbuck before my ex-wife Jenny inadvertently caught Katee's audition on the bedroom TV and scolded me for not seeing how obviously perfect she was."

Others cast members like Aaron Douglas, Michael Hogan, Kandyse McClure, Alessandro Juliani, Nicki Clyne, and Tahmoh Penikett were never approved by any network executives. "These were local, trained actors who ultimately became the show's backbone, with entire story arcs built around them," Eick says. "But they were not the preening, airbrushed Hollywood models you see crowding network crime shows every fall. Had we been forced to crush them through that grueling approval process, I often wonder how many of them—if any—would've made the cut." Thankfully, even without a

ABOVE: In the reimagined series a set of new faces went with some familiar (and not-so-familiar) names. From left to right: James Callis (Gaius Baltar), Tricia Helfer (Number Six), Michael Hogan (Saul Tigh), Mary McDonnell (Laura Roslin), Edward James Olmos (William Adama), Jamie Bamber (Lee "Apollo" Adama), Aaron Douglas (Galen Tyrol), Grace Park (Sharon "Boomer" Valerii), Katee Sackhoff (Kara "Starbuck" Thrace).

hold option, those actors were all available to return for the series

that followed.

"The weirdest thing about the *Battlestar Galactica* cast was how

huge the bandwidth of experience among them was," Eick says. "It

seems virtually every show these days has 'stars' playing against

unknown actors, but the chasm separating those two categories on

Battlestar was unbelievable. We had multiple Oscar nominees Edward

James Olmos and Mary McDonnell in scenes with people who were

literally doing their first or second professional jobs. Ever. I'm going

from memory here, but I believe at the time we cast Tricia Helfer, she

had only performed in a single episode of *CSI*. As a dead body."

The larger-than-average cast of *Battlestar Galactica* with its

award-winning actors working alongside relative unknowns could

have experienced any number of problems from egos to insecurities

and everything in between. Eick proudly proclaims that the person-

alities that had come together in the casting room arrived with none

of that baggage and didn't pick it up along the way. "Ordinarily,

that kind of experience or 'fame discrepancy' could well create big

ABOVE: Minor characters in the miniseries, from left to right: Gaeta (Alessandro Juliani), Helo (Tahmoh Penikett), and Dualla (Kandyse McClure) would go on to play major roles in the series that followed.

problems in almost no time as the novelty of a new series being produced in a foreign country wears off, and a kings versus peasants fiefdom dynamic threatens to set in. But because of the kind of people that Eddie and Mary are, there was never so much as a hint of that."

To this day, Eick speaks of his leads with a reverence that borders on awe. "Mary is the kind of actor whose approach to the craft truly moves you, even as you watch her performance live, on set," he says. "Curmudgeonly cynics working their umpteenth TV series would still crowd around the monitor when she was doing a take. She had star power even among her peers—but with a kindness and a genuine intellectual curiosity that reveals an honest vulnerability. That rubbed off. People felt like they could trust Mary, and so they started trusting each other. The stereotype is true that actors as good as Mary can often be like thoroughbred race horses: amazing to watch, but high-strung, temperamental, volatile. It's the opposite with her, and that's a rare thing. As they say, God usually doesn't give with both hands."

Eick's praise continues for the other half of the fleet's leadership. "You've heard the cliché: when a movie star takes a TV series gig, he tortures everyone around him out of humiliation that he's not a movie star anymore. It's a cliché because it's usually true. And Edward James Olmos—as much a social/political luminary as an international star—could have looked at doing *Battlestar Galactica* for Syfy as some symbol of career oblivion. Instead, he did the opposite. Eddie would look you in the eye and tell you that doing *Battlestar Galactica* in Vancouver for Syfy in 2004 was, quite simply, the finest thing an actor could be doing. *And he meant it.* A lot of it was due to his humble theater training but it wasn't just that. He loved the shit out of those scripts. It invigorated him and, I believe, tapped into a reservoir of talent and commitment that may have surprised even him. His passion for it was so genuine that it was just really, really difficult for anyone else to act like an asshole."

David Eick isn't one to sugarcoat things. So, when he continues to praise the actors who would go from miniseries to series with him as being genuine and hardworking, it's easy to believe that he's telling the truth. "Our cast was made up of mostly young, sexy kids who had never done a series before," he says. "Along with Canadian soap stars, local dinner theater actors, journeymen who'd been struggling through showbiz since the Carter administration. And when overnight they're in *Rolling Stone Magazine* and *The New Yorker* and have their faces plastered on the sides of buildings, that can quickly become a magic carpet to Asshole City. But it never happened. *Prima donna* was a four-letter word on that set. Over a five-year period, I can count on one hand the number of times I had to 'get an actor out of his trailer' because of some tantrum or breakdown. That's unheard of with an ensemble cast as large and eclectic as ours. But everyone thought they were lucky to be there. And I attribute a ton of that to the tone Eddie and Mary set. The fish stinks from the head."

RIGHT: Costume designer Glenne Campbell and illustrator Terry Pitts contributed to the look of the reimagined series' character apparel and developed the looks shown here (left to right): Deckhand, Young Adama, Starbuck, Ellen Tigh, and Selloi.

DECKHAND
BATTLESTAR GALACTICA
Season 4 Episode 1/2
Costume Designer
GLENNE CAMPBELL

TPitts 07

YOUNG ADAMA
BATTLESTAR GALACTICA
Season 4 Episode 1/2
Costume Designer
GLENNE CAMPBELL

TPitts
05/07

"KARA"
BATTLESTAR GALACTICA

COSTUME DESIGNER
GLENNE CAMPBELL
NOVEMBER 2005

ELLEN
Battlestar Galactica
Season 4 Episode 417
Costume Designer
Glenne Campbell

Selloi
Battlestar Galactica
season 3 episode 3
Costume Designer Glenne Campbell

BATTLESTAR GALACTICA:
Naturalistic Science Fiction or Taking the *Opera* Out of Space Opera

(a.k.a. "The Manifesto")

In the early years of the new millennium, genre shows were still a struggle to produce on television. No matter how much a small contingent of critics and loyal fans would support a *Star Trek* series or shows like *Buffy the Vampire Slayer,* anything that was outside of the realm of traditional dramas or comedies were a tough sell in Hollywood. Actors were reluctant to take on roles that would potentially typecast them, making it harder to get future jobs. These shows were largely ignored during awards season, except for the technical categories. A decade later there are noticeably more science-fiction series on the air, but they still don't always get the critical respect and audience attention they deserve.

The incremental changes that have occurred over time in the entertainment industry's interest in genre television are partially due to the success of *Battlestar Galactica*, but in 2003 the series hadn't happened yet, so no one had seen what they intended to do. Once Moore was finished with the miniseries script, Eick suggested that he add a brief sales piece to the document explaining their vision to the network. Even though Syfy had already approved the initial pitch, this was a little extra insurance to make sure executives were on the same page with their concept should the miniseries be a success.

Moore created a three-page document entitled "Battlestar Galactica: Naturalistic Science Fiction or Taking the *Opera* Out of Space Opera" and sent it off with little thought of who would be reading it. The "manifesto," as it became known, laid out in clear detail exactly how the documentary-style of filming would ground it in a dramatic reality that wasn't typically associated with genre television among the mass audience.

The script made the rounds to the studio with that document still attached, as it would be when it was sent out for casting as well. Edward James Olmos was among the actors being considered for the role of Adama, but he wasn't initially interested in the part. Even though the actor already had a diverse résumé, includes everything from *Miami Vice* and *The West Wing* to voice work in *Beverly Hills Chihuahua*, he had the usual concerns about being associated with a so-called space opera. But getting established actors like Olmos and Mary McDonnell to headline the series would lend to the gravitas in tone the producers were hoping to achieve. Thanks to Eick's suggestion to create a manifesto, that particular challenge became a lot easier.

As Olmos mentions in the DVD commentary for *Battlestar Galactica* Season 4.5, he'd brought the miniseries script along with him while on a book tour, but he wasn't sure that he was even going to look at it. It was his wife who picked up the script during some downtime and read Moore's three-page introduction. After that, she told him he had to read it. Eick and Moore had no clue what the actor was talking about when he credited that introduction with getting him interested in the project. They hadn't even realized it had gone out with the script.

RIGHT: The series pitch credited with bringing the franchise to a new generation of viewers.

NATURALISTIC SCIENCE FICTION
OR
TAKING THE OPERA OUT OF SPACE OPERA

Our goal is nothing less than the reinvention of the science fiction television series.

We take as a given the idea that the traditional space opera, with its stock characters, techno-double-talk, bumpy-headed aliens, thespian histrionics, and empty heroics has run its course and a new approach is required. That approach is to introduce realism into what has heretofore been an aggressively unrealistic genre.

Call it "Naturalistic Science Fiction."

This idea, the presentation of a fantastical situation in naturalistic terms, will permeate every aspect of our series:

Visual. The first thing that will leap out at viewers is the dynamic use of the documentary or cinema verite style. Through the extensive use of hand-held cameras, practical lighting, and functional set design, the battlestar Galactica will feel on every level like a real place.

This shift in tone and look cannot be overemphasized. It is our intention to deliver a show that does not look like any other science fiction series ever produced. A casual viewer should for a moment feel like he or she has accidently surfed onto a "60 Minutes" documentary piece about life aboard an aircraft carrier until someone starts talking about Cylons and battlestars.

That is not to say we're shooting on videotape under fluorescent lights, but we will be striving for a verisimilitude that is sorely lacking in virtually every other science fiction series ever attempted. We're looking for filmic truth, not manufactured "pretty pictures" or the "way cool" factor.

Perhaps nowhere will this be more surprising than in our visual effects shots. Our ships will be treated like real ships that someone had to go out and film with a real camera. That means no 3-D "hero" shots panning and zooming wildly with the touch of a mousepad. The questions we will ask before every VFX shot are things like: "How did we get this shot? Where is the camera? Who's holding it? Is the cameraman in another spacecraft? Is the camera mounted on the wing?" This philosophy will generate images that will present an audience jaded and bored with the same old "Wow -- it's a CGI shot!" with a different texture and a different cinematic language that will force them to re-evaluate their notions of science fiction.

Our visual style will also capitalize on the possibilities inherent in the series concept itself to deliver unusual imagery not typically seen in this genre. That is, the inclusion of a variety of civilian ships each of which will have unique properties and visual references that can be in stark contrast to the military life aboard Galactica. For example, we have a vessel in our rag-tag fleet which was designed to be a space-going marketplace or "City Walk" environment. The juxtaposition of this high-gloss, sexy atmosphere against the gritty reality of a story for survival will give us more textures and levels to play than in typical genre fare.

EDITORIAL. Our style will avoid the now cliched MTV fast-cutting while at the same time foregoing Star Trek's somewhat ponderous and lugubrious "master, two-shot, close-up, close-up, two-shot, back to master" pattern. If there is a model here, it would be vaguely Hitchcockian -- that is, a sense of building suspense and dramatic tension through the use of extending takes and long masters which pull the audience into the reality of the action rather than the distract through the use of ostentatious cutting patterns.

STORY. We will eschew the usual stories about parallel universes, time-travel, mindcontrol, evil twins, God-like powers and all the other cliches of the genre. Our show is first and foremost a drama. It is about people. Real people that the audience can identify with and become engaged in. It is not a show about hardware or bizarre alien cultures. It is a show about us. It is an allegory for our own society, our own people and it should be immediately recognizable to any member of the audience.

SCIENCE. Our spaceships don't make noise because there is no noise in space. Sound will be provided from sources inside the ships -- the whine of an engine audible to the pilot for instance. Our fighters are not airplanes and they will not be shackled by the conventions of WWII dogfights. The speed of light is a law and there will be no moving violations.

And finally, **CHARACTER.** This is perhaps, the biggest departure from the science fiction norm. We do not have "the cocky guy" "the fast-talker" "the brain" "the wacky alien sidekick" or any of the other usual characters who populate a space series.

Our characters are living, breathing people with all the emotional complexity and contradictions present in quality dramas like "The West Wing" or "The Sopranos." In this way, we hope to challenge our audience in ways that other genre pieces do not. We want the audience to connect with the characters of *Galactica* as people. Our characters are not super-heroes. They are not an elite. They are everyday people caught up in a enormous cataclysm and trying to survive it as best they can.

THEY ARE YOU AND ME.

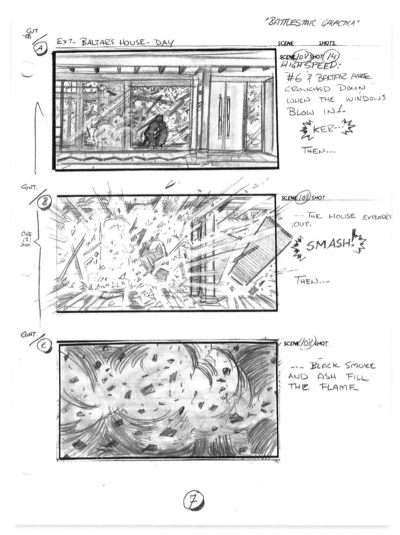

LEFT: Storyboards lay out the visuals for the miniseries scene in which Gaius Baltar learns the devastating truth from Six as nuclear bombs ravage Caprica, destroying Baltar's home in the process.

THE JOURNEY
BEGINS AGAIN

The *Battlestar Galactica* miniseries aired over two nights on December 8 and 9 in 2003, ending with the cliffhanger reveal that Sharon "Boomer" Valerii (Grace Park) was a Cylon. The producers had approached the two-night event with their eyes on a series order. The very nature of the show following a fleet on a journey toward Earth meant that the story would not be resolved at the end of the second episode. They had to leave audiences wanting more. The question was would there be enough of an audience in the first place?

The first night the miniseries aired, it garnered an acceptable, if not blockbuster, 3.2 Nielsen rating. As audiences for most television premieres tend to decline between the first and second episode, the producers figured they could survive a small drop in viewership for the second night and still receive an order for more episodes from the network. With the miniseries airing on Syfy, a cable network, the numbers did not need to be as high as traditional network television. But, like the original series, they did have to meet a threshold that would justify the cost of the production. Everyone from the network to the producers was pleasantly surprised when the Nielsen ratings for the second night of the series came in and the numbers had *risen* to a 3.8.

"The ratings were solid, but unspectacular," David Eick admits. A series order was not immediately in the cards, but an opportunity of a different sort was for Eick. "Shortly afterward, I was offered a senior executive job at Universal TV," he says, "which I definitely did not want. I wanted to get a *Battlestar* series greenlit and I wanted to produce that show. However, there seemed to be an opportunity to get inside the bureaucratic machine that would determine my show's fate, so with the understanding that I could leave at any time without consequence, I accepted the 'suit' job."

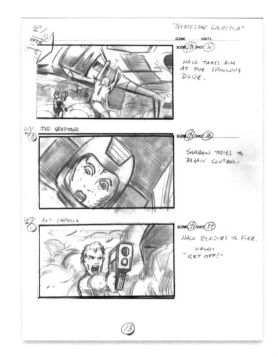

"BATTLESTAR GALACTICA"

SCENE 14 SHOT 35
HALO TAKES AIM AT THE SPINNING DUDE.

SCENE 14 SHOT 36
SHARON TRIES TO REGAIN CONTROL.

SCENE 14 SHOT 37
HALO READIES TO FIRE.
HALO: "GET OFF!"

13

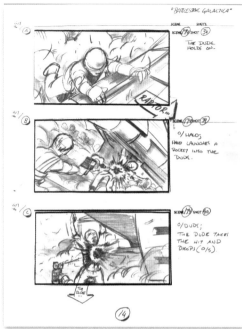

"BATTLESTAR GALACTICA"

SCENE 14 SHOT 38
THE DUDE HOLDS ON.

SCENE 14 SHOT 39
O/ HALO;
HALO LAUNCHES A ROCKET INTO THE DUDE.

SCENE 14 SHOT 40
O/DUDE;
THE DUDE TAKES THE HIT AND DROPS (O/S).

14

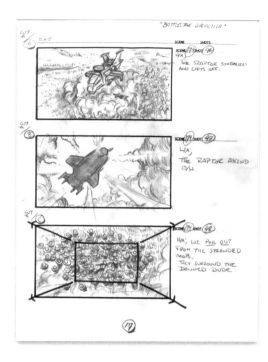

"BATTLESTAR GALACTICA"

SCENE 14 SHOT 41
HAS;
THE RAPTOR STABILIZES AND LIFTS OFF.

SCENE 14 SHOT 42
HAS;
THE RAPTOR ASCENDS O/H.

SCENE 14 SHOT 43
HAS; WE PULL OUT FROM THE STRANDED MOB.
THEY SURROUND THE DOWNED DUDE.

15

Shortly after the miniseries' debut, Michael Jackson, the head of cable television for Universal, passed on a one-hour series pickup. The series budget was deemed too expensive given the ratings expectations, and, as Eick explains, "No yelling or begging or gnashing of teeth could convince him otherwise. I was devastated. I shook every tree I could find, but it seemed doomed."

All, however, was not lost. Belinda Menendez, the head of Universal TV's International division, made a proposal to Eick that changed everything. She proposed that if they could grant SKY TV—a UK network, where the *Battlestar* miniseries was quite well-received—world premiere rights, Sky would contribute an episodic stipend that would lower Universal's financial risk and make the show a more interesting financial proposition.

"The trick was persuading Jackson to allow another foreign network the bragging rights to a world premiere of a U.S. show," Eick says. "But as an expat Brit himself, Jackson seemed more than happy to share the glory in exchange for the financial booster shot. And it was done: *Battlestar*—the *series*—was a go." As a studio executive with a discretionary budget, Eick immediately made a deal with Ron Moore to come aboard, and then promptly resigned his studio job and joined him.

The first series episode of *Battlestar Galactica*, "33," aired ten months after the miniseries in the UK and three months later in the US (along with the second episode "Water" in a two-hour premiere event). Going from a miniseries to a full slate of episodes required numerous changes seen on-screen and off. Ron Moore left *Carnivale* to focus full-time on the new series with David Eick and the production team. Many people from the production would return, while some fresh blood came in as well. Actors who had smaller roles in the miniseries would become more fully fleshed out characters, including Tahmoh Penikett (Karl "Helo" Agathon), who had so impressed the producers that they asked him back even though the original intention was to leave Helo on Caprica, never to be heard from again. One of the most

LEFT: In shots that closely mirror the storyboard layout, Helo (Tahmoh Penikett) protects the Raptor as pilot Boomer (Grace Park) leaves Caprica with a small number of refugees, including Gaius Baltar.

notable additions to the ongoing series was Richard Hatch, the original Apollo, in the role of Tom Zarek.

Richard Hatch has admitted to being disappointed in Universal's decision to "reimagine" the series that had made him a household name for a time. He'd felt that the story of the original Colonial fleet should continue instead. With the political changes in the world and the dramatic shifts in television narrative, it could allow *Galactica* to become the more thought-provoking, less "escapist" series he'd always wanted it to be. As a viewer, he approached the new miniseries with trepidation, not entirely falling for it at first, but accepting that this was the future of the series he'd been tied to for decades.

It was during a meeting with Ron Moore at the 2003 Galacticon convention celebrating the twenty-fifth anniversary of the original series that Hatch began to come around. The convention occurred a couple of months before the miniseries aired so Hatch was still cautious about the idea. But he appreciated the direction Moore said the production was planning to take the material in, exploring modern-day issues mirrored through a science-fiction reflection. Months later, when an offer for a role in the series was extended, Hatch accepted.

The first season of the reimagined *Battlestar Galactica* continued to distinguish itself from the original series in dealing with the realities of fleeing from the Cylons in search of a new home. This was aided by the important decision to make the show serialized rather than episodic.

In episodic television, each storyline is largely contained to a single episode with the events rarely impacting future stories. By contrast, a serialized episode will clearly have a beginning, middle, and end, but it is designed as part of an overall continuing story. The impact of a decision made in one moment can play out over several episodes, color various storylines, and even come back later in the life of the series. This allowed the writers and actors to explore the challenges of

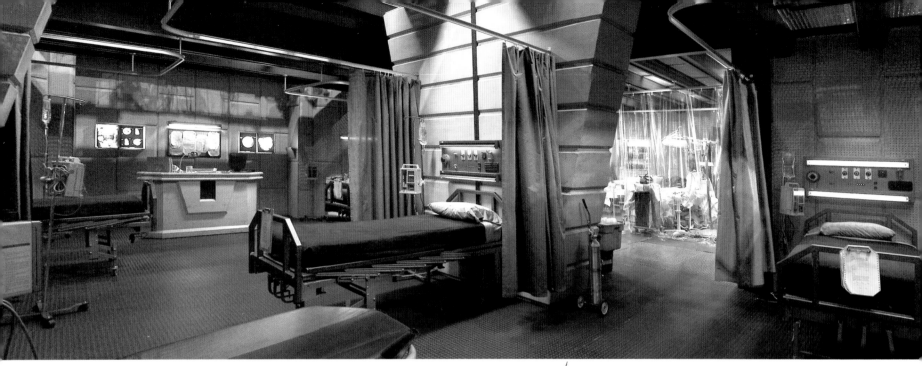

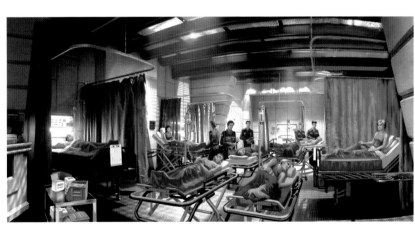

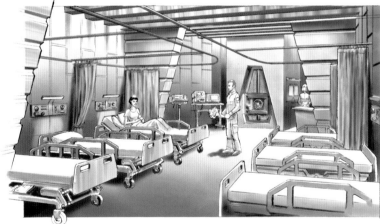

ABOVE: The *Galactica* sickbay, like much of the ship, had a more functional design than traditional space operas. Ken Rabehl's concept sketches reveal a more ward-like sickbay and how the space could be used for triage when needed.

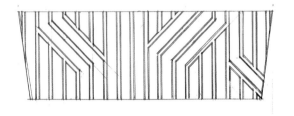

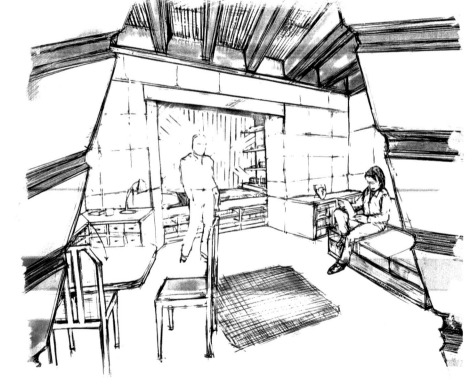

THIS PAGE: The styling of *Galactica* blended a nautical design with a battleship aesthetic as seen in concept art and set photos of William Adama's office (top left, bottom left) and the officer's quarters (top center, top right, bottom right).

the seemingly endless journey on the emotional state of the characters and its physical impact on the ship.

"It was very important to *Galactica* because of the nature of our story," Moore explains. "One of the fundamental problems with the original series was that they pretty much were not allowed to serialize the story. Each episode kind of had to be a one-off. But at the same time, the conceptual framework of the show was *Galactica* going someplace, heading in some direction with the same group of people on these same ships. It sort of had to be a continuing story on some level. But they really, strongly resisted [that] in the old [series] and there's a sort of scattershot approach to what elements of continuity there are and are not." The first season of *Battlestar Galactica* premiered the same year as *Lost* and both shows would play an important role in changing the nature of storytelling on television.

Prior to 2004, most TV shows were episodic in nature, allowing viewers to skip an episode without missing major developments in the ongoing story. An example of the difference in storytelling opportunities can be seen in a series Ron Moore was briefly involved with, *Star Trek: Voyager*. On *Voyager*, another crew was also taking a long space journey in search of Earth, but the challenges they faced rarely continued past an hour. This was reportedly a network edict because executives did not want to impact the potential syndication deal where episodes could air out of order without confusing audiences. Almost a decade had passed between *Voyager*'s premiere and *Galactica*, but Moore faced the same type of network reticence.

"With us," Moore continues, "I said from the very beginning, 'Look, there is a continuing story here.' And I placated the network in the beginning by saying, 'But of course we can always do an A-B-C structure.' Where an A-story is going to be episodic. 'This week's A-story will begin and end with the main character—like this is a Starbuck show and we'll have this Starbuck storyline that begins and ends in the show. But then on the B-level we're going to have

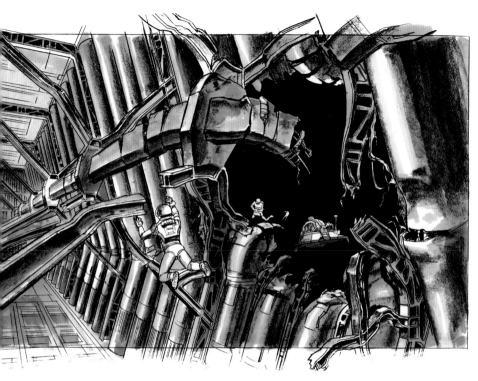

continuing stories of individual characters that might last two or three episodes. And then on the C-level there's going to be the longer-term story of the fleet or Roslin/Adama, where they're going, the big mythology.' That was how I sold it to them, even though I kind of knew it was going to be more serialized than that."

In the new millennium, the packaging of television series was already evolving. Additional outlets were being created to extend the life of a TV show on DVD and later online streaming. "Binge-watching" became a term to describe people who mainlined an entire season in a weekend of viewing. Suddenly continuing stories with ongoing

plots were all the rage, and *Battlestar Galactica* played an important role in that evolution of television viewing, though it was not always a smooth ride. "As [serialized stories] got more popular and as other shows started to gain momentum that did that format, it became easier," Moore admits. "But pretty much during *Galactica*'s whole run—except in the final season—there was a constant back-and-forth with the network. They would really have preferred that there was a much stronger episodic structure even at that point because they were more comfortable with it."

PICTURED: The serial format of *Battlestar Galactica* permitted the multi-season development of characters like Galen Tyrol as seen in concept art and stills from "Water" (season one, episode 2), in which Chief leads a reconnaissance mission into a sabotaged water tanker (opposite page), and "Blood on the Scales" (season four, episode 14), in which Tyrol, now a known Cylon, remains loyal to William Adama and Laura Roslin, disabling the *Galactica*'s FTL drive during the Gaeta-Zarek mutiny (this page).

"33"

Written by: Ronald D. Moore
Directed by: Michael Rymer

The Colonial fleet prepares to spool up its Faster-Than-Light (FTL) Drive for the two hundred thirty-seventh jump in a row in the past five days. No matter where they have jumped to, no matter how far they have traveled from home, every thirty-three minutes the Cylons find them and attack. When one of the ships in the fleet, the *Olympic Carrier*, fails to make the next jump and the Cylons do not attack, the *Galactica* crew assumes it is due to the missing ship. Later, when the *Carrier* reappears on a destructive path showing signs of a nuclear weapon and refuses to answer hails, Apollo is forced to shoot it down under the assumption that all onboard are already lost.

"33" won the 2005 Hugo Award for Best Dramatic Presentation, Short Form and it set the standard for *Battlestar Galactica* episodes to follow. Years later, after the series had ended, Ron Moore would still consider it the single episode he was most proud of. "It was so out there and different," he says. "And it felt like it was a really great way to kick off season one with a really unusual structure. It was just a great writing experience because I wrote it without an outline. I just sat down and started writing and it just flowed. And that was a rare thing."

Moore had written the episode over Christmas break after the mini-series had aired. Syfy was still unsure about an episode order for the show, but another player in the form of the now defunct UPN network expressed interest. But the new network would at least need to see the script of a future episode to get an idea of where the series would go. David Eick called up Moore to ask if he could quickly produce one and the writer got to work, pulling the idea randomly out of some log lines for potential episodes they had discussed if the show went to series. "I just wrote the script and turned it in as a way of selling the show to another network," Moore says. "And it became the first episode." Syfy did eventually place that order for a thirteen-episode season with "33" airing in the US on January 14, 2005.

The story of "33" picks up only days after the miniseries ended with the opening scenes revealing exhaustion in the faces of the fleet. This provides a few minutes of mystery for the audience trying to figure out what is going on as they have come in at the middle of the action. It is the first real hint that the story of *Battlestar Galactica* continues, occurring before *and* after the viewers have tuned in and will not just be neatly resolved in an hour.

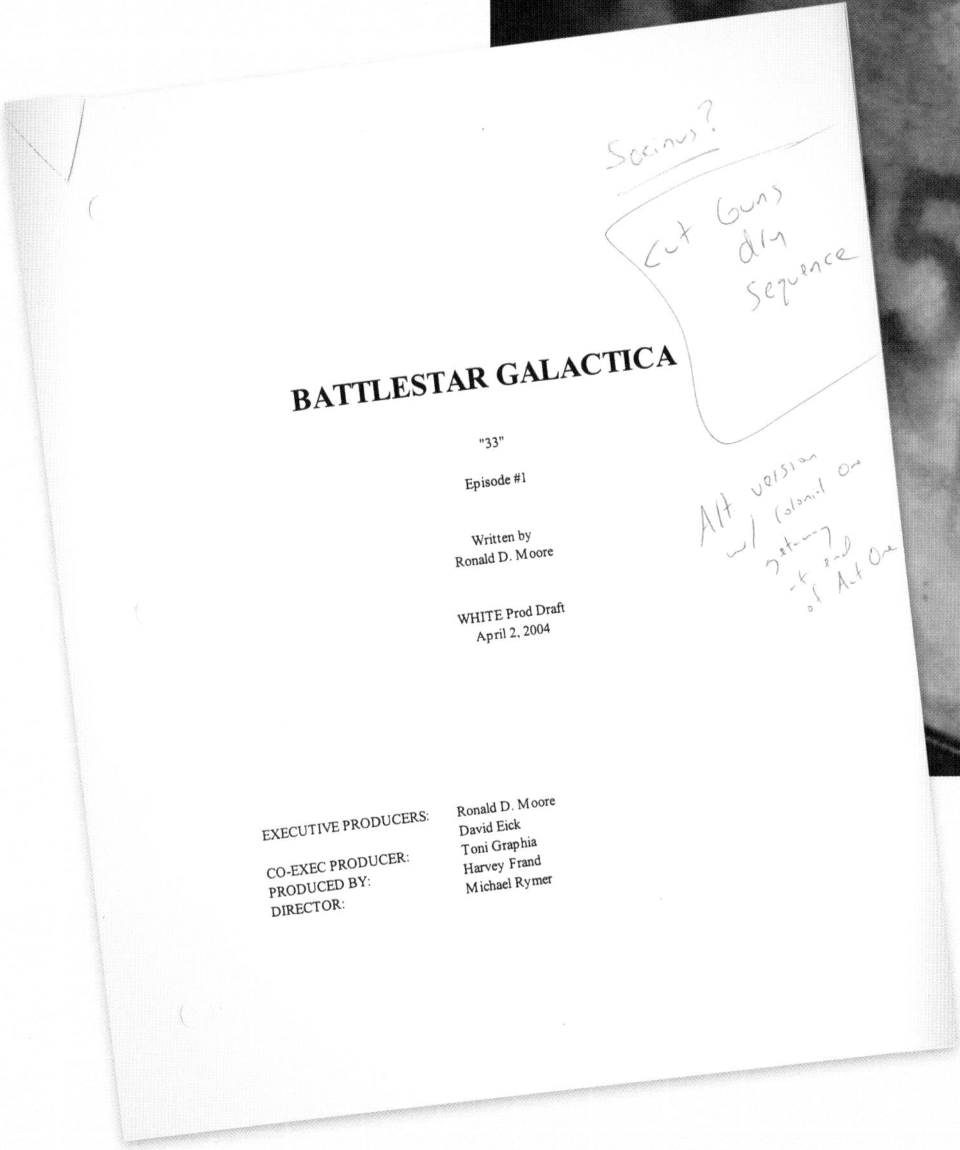

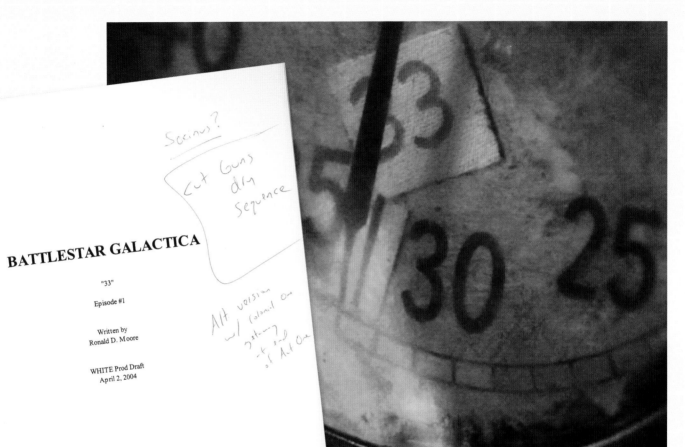

BATTLESTAR GALACTICA

"33"

Episode #1

Written by
Ronald D. Moore

WHITE Prod Draft
April 2, 2004

EXECUTIVE PRODUCERS:	Ronald D. Moore
	David Eick
	Toni Graphia
CO-EXEC PRODUCER:	Harvey Frand
PRODUCED BY:	Michael Rymer
DIRECTOR:	

Handwritten notes:

Serious?

Cut Guns dry sequence

Alt version w/ Colonial One Story — at end of Act One

PICTURED: Ron Moore's script for "33," the first hour-long episode of the series, contains notes to himself from script meetings and discussions with the network.

FINDING AN
AUDIENCE

The reimagined *Battlestar Galactica* had a little something for every viewer: action-packed battles, callouts to Earth's history, soap opera elements, and religious allegory presented with a science-fiction twist. The show continued to grow in popularity, although the Nielsen ratings did not always reflect the large audience.

Another important shift in television viewing was occurring throughout *Battlestar Galactica*'s time on the air, affecting the way the success of a show was perceived. For decades, high Nielsen ratings were the Holy Grail, as the more people who tuned in to an episode, the more the network could charge advertisers to run commercials during the broadcast. But with the advent of DVRs that could skip through commercials and DVD boxed sets for marathon viewing, audiences weren't necessarily beholden to sit in front of the TV set the moment an episode of a television show hit the air.

Certainly, some people had other things to do on Friday nights. So as the audience for the show continued to build, it wasn't necessarily reflected in the reports that came back to Syfy.

The network often cited the ratings in their ongoing discussions to cut back on the serialization of the series to avoid losing more of the audience. To the producers, it was an understandable concern, but one that did not mesh with the modern realities of television. "They were worried about people who missed an episode tuning in and being lost," Ron Moore explains. "They were always terrified that if somebody tuned in and they hadn't seen last week's episode, they'd be lost and they'd just turn off the show."

At that point, DVR penetration was still relatively low and nobody was counting the ratings from DVRs in those days. "There was no such thing as live-plus-three or plus-seven," Moore goes on. "The Nielsens weren't tracking it and the advertisers certainly weren't paying anything for it. The networks didn't care about how many times somebody watched it or when they might have viewed it later. We would see the ratings come in and were starting to get some data about it, but it was very preliminary data. If you included the numbers from DVRs we were getting like thirty to forty percent higher ratings ... DVR is what makes serialized programming work. Your ability to bank a few episodes or to record the ones that you missed or to go back and find them online takes away the fear that 'Oh, I'll be lost if I tune in on episode four.'"

With popularity for *Battlestar Galactica* growing in various formats, Syfy still strongly believed in the franchise and increased the episode order to twenty for the second season. This was almost as much as the standard twenty-two to twenty-four episode season traditionally found on network television. In what was rare at the time and has become commonplace today, that second season was marked by a three-month break after the tenth episode aired. The benefit of such a structure not only spread

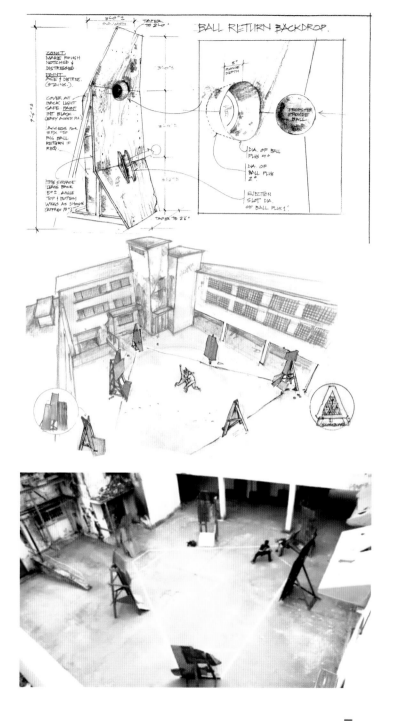

RIGHT: The Pyramid game came together through sketches and plans to create an important tie to the original series—when the game was called Triad—and an even more direct connection to life before the fall of the colonies.

out the season in a way that allowed the episodes to air largely without reruns, but it also initiated what has become known as the mid-season finale, another concept *Galactica* pioneered that is commonplace today.

The sophomore season ended with the second episode of the two-part finale "Lay Down Your Burdens," in which another dramatic shift occurred in the fleet with the election of Gaius Baltar as president and the discovery of a habitable—if not entirely hospitable—planet. Nothing in the story, however, would generate as much discussion as the decision to jump ahead a year and a half in the midst of the episode. This would become another common trope in television in the ensuing years, but was nearly unheard-of at the time. The time jump allowed for drastic changes in the characters' lives post-flight from the Cylons, only to end with the cliff-hanger of the hated enemies invading their "New Caprica."

PICTURED: The matte painting of the New Caprica landscape as viewed from Baltar's window on *Colonial One* began as a concept sketch by storyboard artist David MacLean.

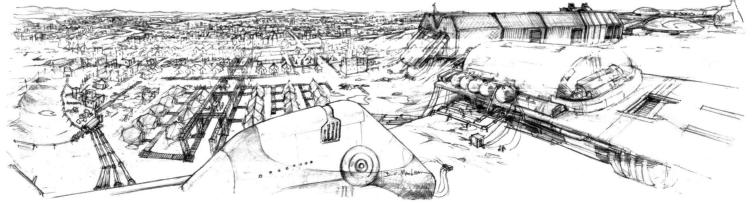

"THE LIVING LEGEND" / "PEGASUS"

"The Living Legend, Parts 1 and 2"
Teleplay by: Glen A. Larson
Story by: Ken Pettus and Glen A. Larson
Directed by: Vince Edwards

"Pegasus"

Written by: Anne Cofell Saunders
Directed by: Michael Rymer

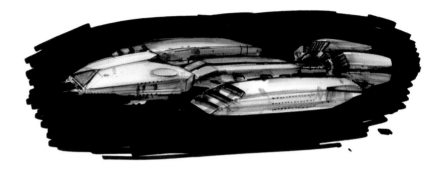

The Colonial fleet receives a welcome surprise in the original series two-part episodes "The Living Legend" when it reunites with another surviving battlestar thought to have been lost during the Cylon attack. The lone *Battlestar Pegasus*, under the leadership of the legendary Commander Cain, has taken every opportunity to inflict damage on the Cylons while Adama has focused on avoiding risky encounters and defending the fleet as they searched for Earth. Tensions quickly rise between the crews of the ships when the two different command styles clash, but they eventually unite in a plan to attack the Cylons while obtaining the needed fuel for the fleet. The risk is a success, but the *Pegasus* and Cain are lost in the melee.

The original series two-part episode of "The Living Legend" was notable for the inclusion of special guest star Lloyd Bridges in the titular role of Admiral Cain and the addition of Anne Lockhart to the cast as his daughter, Sheba. It was a standout storyline in the series and a fan favorite. The ambiguous ending, in which the fleet is unsure whether or not the *Pegasus* survived, left the story open for the writers to bring the ship back, which was the intention had the series continued. In another two-part original series episode, "War of the Gods," Count Iblis tells Sheba that she will see her father again, suggesting that he is alive.

Decades later, the reimagined series would chart its own course to Earth, with nods to the original throughout the journey. The second season episode "Pegasus" was one of the most direct homages

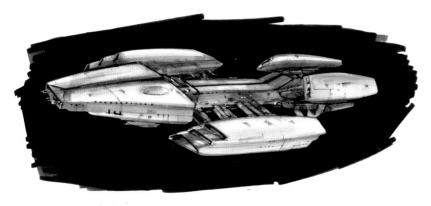

undertaken by the writers, mirroring the storyline of the battlestar reunion with its own darker twists. It was a risk to approach such a beloved episode, but one that paid off for the series by bringing a new dynamic to the fleet and mixing up the relationships between the characters in much the same way the original did.

Both the original and reimagined series episodes dealt with the challenges facing the crew of a lone battlestar believing it is the last of a once powerful fleet of ships. The approach each episode took revealed the dramatic differences between the two shows, while also highlighting what they had in common. The *Pegasus* crew in the re-imagined series went to a much darker place than their predecessors had in the original episode. The crew on *Pegasus* has intentionally stranded survivors that Michelle Forbes's version of Admiral Cain

has deemed superfluous to their cause and has treated their Cylon prisoner in inhumane ways.

In light of events in the real world, the harsh treatment of prisoners was a topic in the news, following Abu Ghraib, and could be properly reflected through a science-fiction mirror. At the same time, the basis for this story was universal and could be found in "The Living Legend" when Lloyd Bridges's Cain is consumed with taking revenge on the Cylons in much the same way Captain Ahab is focused on his white whale of Moby Dick.

PICTURED: David MacLean's design concepts for the *Pegasus* incorporated the aesthetic of the *Galactica* while updating it for the more modern spacecraft which had received a technological overhaul that the titular ship of the series had not.

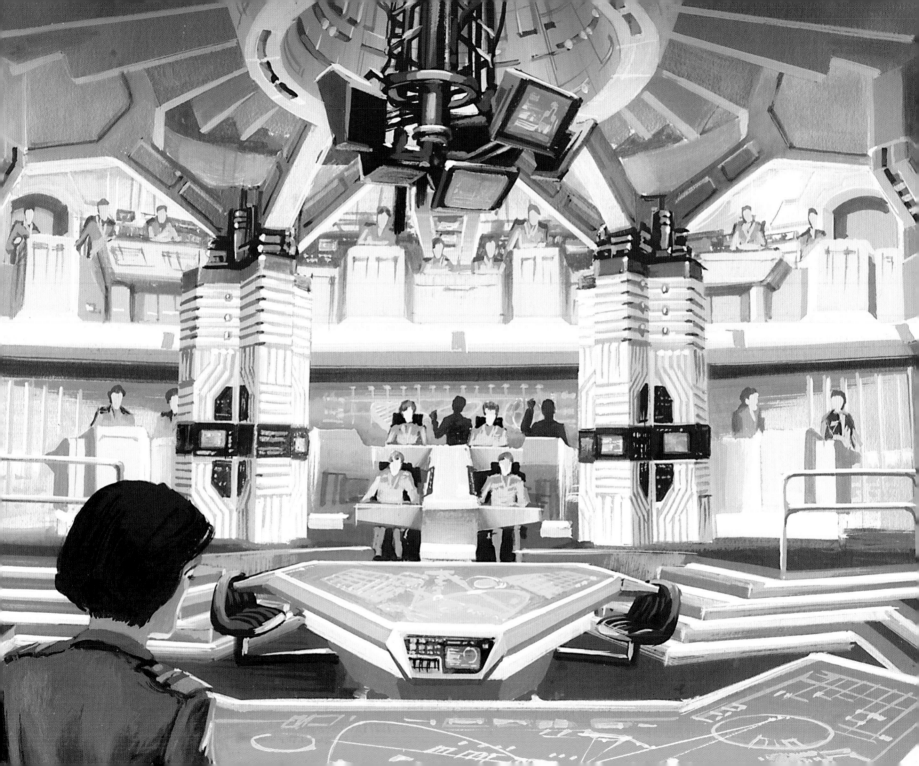

THE SECOND EXODUS

The core concept of both *Battlestar Galactica* series was the journey of that ragtag fleet to the shining planet known as Earth. When the second season of the reimagined version ended with the Colonials setting up their home on a new planet that was not Earth, it was almost guaranteed that they would eventually find themselves back in space one day. But while they were on the planet, the production had the opportunity to test out another new concept in television viewing: the webisode.

The online streaming of web series—short episodes airing online that are set in the universe of a television show—was one of the growing list of ways audiences could enjoy their favorite shows outside of the ongoing storyline. A series of webisodes starring several cast members under the title *Battlestar Galactica: The Resistance* revealed what life was like for the Colonials on New Caprica in the lead up to

LEFT: The original concept for the Command Information Center (CIC) seen in Ken Rabehl's sketches kept some of the levels in the final design, but changed the layout during development.

RIGHT: Once the CIC was complete it, along with many other *Galactica* sets, was deemed too clean and neat and had to be distressed to achieve the look of a soon-to-be decommissioned ship that was getting on in years.

the third season. This "bonus material" fit into the continuity of the se-ries, but was not required viewing for the audience, straddling the line between being a preview for the new season and a complete story in itself. The webisodes were popular enough marketing tools that more web series were created in the future.

"The term 'webisode' was something I'd never heard when we em-barked on *Battlestar Galactica*," David Eick admits. "But they proved to be a surprise success and an opportunistic vehicle for a couple reasons: First, it was the brainchild of the underrated marketing team at Syfy, who never stopped cooking up new and innovative ways to promote the show. This is crucial for a producer, since any risky or speculative endeavor like this, which becomes successful, only further impregnates your studio and network partners. Of course it's their 'job' to keep your show on the air, but all of a sudden they start *personally* wanting your show to succeed, because they're seeing some of their own ideas come to winning fruition.

"Secondly, webisodes became an invaluable 'farm league' for our cast and crew: We wrote for the actors who had the neces-sary free time, which meant that borderline characters we might have neglected due to lack of imagination suddenly had a forum to showcase their talents in ways we'd never see otherwise, which in turn led to future opportunities on *Battlestar*. Also, our policy for the webisodes' production was to promote from within; everyone got to move up a rank—so the 'baby writer' (or writer's assistant) got to write something that would actually see the light of day; the gaffer got to be the D.P.; the P.A. became the assistant director; the assistant director finally got his shot to direct, etcetera. Before long, a whole other tier of talent was being developed who would find future opportunities on *Battlestar Galactica, Caprica,* and other projects even years later."

The third season that followed those webisodes stuck to a more tra-ditional airing schedule, beginning with a two-hour premiere combining the episodes "Occupation" and "Precipice." These stories would lead up to the two-part "Exodus" episode that would once again see the fleet on the move. That episode, in particular, was notable for what became known as the Adama Maneuver, in which Admiral Adama jumps *Galactica* into the planet's atmosphere, a visual effects tour de force that had fans debating the logistics of the complex move. But no one questioned the visual effects artistry required to create the look of the ship bursting through the atmosphere.

To this day, the producers rave over the work of the visual effects team for their contributions to the entire series. "It was an amazing, amazing team," Ron Moore enthusiastically states. "We started with Zoic Studios, and Gary Hutzel was our visual effects supervisor. As the show progressed, Gary just kept building an internal visual effects unit that became our in-house unit. Once we had the in-house unit, we could really go because the cost savings were enormous. We had complete control over the entire line of production. We got a lot more

RIGHT: This set (from concept to reality) shows the after effects of the explosion in the New Caprica Police Academy in "Occupation" with production designer Richard Hudolin's vision as drawn by assistant art director Ivana Vasak.

shots generated. We could really take more passes. It just made it a much better operation."

"More importantly," Eick adds, "we could manage the *quality* of those shots much more closely and exhaustively because we weren't in violation of any contractual arrangement limiting the amount of time or effort spent perfecting them. I cannot underscore enough the difference this approach made to the overall presentation. We could accommodate a far greater number of shots per episode, at (in my opinion) a far higher quality. And it didn't cost a penny more than if we'd done it the traditional way.

Moore's enthusiasm mirrors Eick's. "If you look at the show, you can see that the number of effects shots just really takes off by order of magnitudes by the time we get to the last season," Moore says. "We were doing amazing things that were so far beyond our capabilities at the beginning, or far beyond any show's capabilities, I have to say. I don't think there was a show that did more intensive visual effects work than we did. And we did it on a Syfy budget, which

wasn't that much. Gary deserves the lion's share of the credit for the visual effects work on the show overall."

That final season of *Battlestar Galactica* premiered more than a year after the third season ended, but the fans did not have to wait all that time for a new episode. Universal's home video department asked the production team to develop a TV-movie that could air on the network and be released on DVD with additional unaired scenes to enhance the experience. This would help bridge some of the long gap between seasons.

To create an episode airing after what was essentially a cliff-hanger of a season finale without impacting continuity, the producers bounced around a bit in time, presenting an episode largely set on the *Pegasus* and showing some of Admiral Cain's and Lee Adama's time at the helm of the ship. *Battlestar Galactica: Razor* premiered five months before the fourth season aired, bringing with it another series of webisodes tied to that story.

RIGHT: The initial Cylon Basestar concept art for *Razor* hewed closely to the design of the original series, while the interiors were dramatically different from the stylings seen in the 1978 ship.

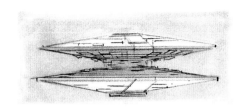

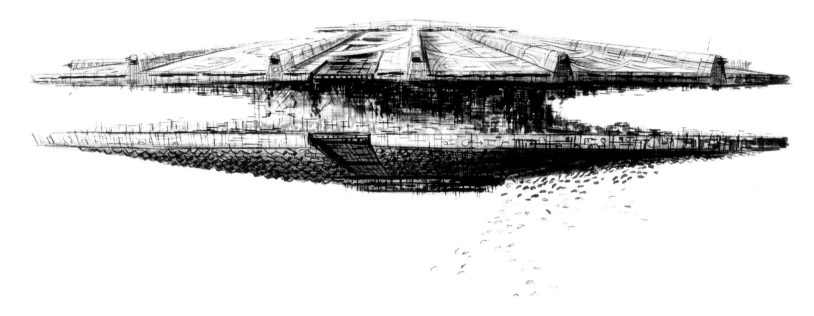

NB: These protruding pieces are to keep the Viper from rolling too far (on our actors)

TICA 757NC

The first official episode of the fourth season, "He That Believeth in Me," arrived on April 4, 2008, ushering in a season with some of the most dramatic and controversial work on the series to date. Starbuck's return from the dead was only one of the mysteries to explore as the mixed crew of the Colonial fleet and Cylon rebels find Earth, only to discover that it is not the home that they have been searching for. The cliff-hanger mid-season finale "Revelations" set up a climactic final run of episodes that aired six months later to reveal the repercussions of the fleet finally losing hope then finding it again and taking sides in the Cylon Civil War.

ABOVE: The scene in which Kara Thrace finds the wreckage of her Viper along with her body in the episode "Sometimes A Great Notion" began as a concept sketch designed by Richard Hudolin and drawn by David MacLean.

When it came time to wrap up the journey of this Colonial fleet, Moore found himself in the awkward position of having too much story to tell and not enough time to tell it. The series, with its large cast of characters, had numerous storylines to tie up, a climactic battle with the Cylons approaching, and several mysteries to solve, including the biggest: with Earth no longer a habitable option, would they ever find a world on which they could settle? The script overflowed with scenes, with much more to do than a two-hour finale could handle, necessitating it to be expanded into three parts.

Developing the finale, "Daybreak," as a three-hour movie gave the production room to breathe. It also allowed them to craft proper endings for all—or most—of the characters. The downside was that Moore's script didn't have a natural break for what would be the end of the first episode. The writer wanted to keep the three hours together for one straight-through viewing, but the network balked, opting to split the first episode out to air on March

13, 2009 with the second and third parts shown a week later as a two-hour movie.

As Moore admitted in the DVD commentary for *Battlestar Galactica* Season 4.5, he found solace in the realization that after its initial airing on the network, future viewers of "Daybreak" would experience it in formats from DVDs to online streaming and would be able to watch the episodes unfold together as the story was originally intended. It was another one of the benefits of this interesting time in television history that *Battlestar Galactica* had found itself a part of.

The conclusion to "Daybreak" aired on March 20, 2009. Finally, the Colonial fleet and a select group of Cylons found a home that they could call Earth. They would settle among the indigenous people with Athena and Helo's daughter, Hera, becoming mitochondrial Eve, the Human-Cylon child from whom Earth's version of humanity would ultimately descend. As the fleet scattered across the planet, each

character had a good-bye moment as the audience finally came to understand how the various Colonial and Cylon practices and beliefs would eventually influence our own history.

But one mystery in the series was intentionally left unsolved: What had Kara Thrace (Katee Sackhoff) become after her return from the dead? Though the series strongly hinted at her being an angel, the question remained unanswered as she merely disappeared in the midst of her final conversation with Lee (Jamie Bamber). Once again,

the Internet was aflame with comments and opinions about Starbuck with many angry about the lack of clear resolution. In a way, it was fitting that the series both began and ended with such strong reactions for one of its central characters.

Years after that final episode, the producers look back on their signature series with a great deal of fondness and pride. "*Battlestar Galactica*, for me, represents the hardest thing in life to pull off," says Eick. "Which is, quite simply, accomplishing what you set out

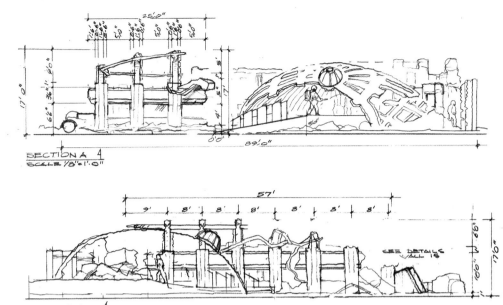

to do. But the takeaway—and this is the boring cliché, but sorry—is the experience and the relationships. The fact that I will never have another time like *Battlestar Galactica* again isn't because the show was perfect—hardly. Far from it, not even close. But that experience, certainly in the beginning, was near perfection in terms of a harmonious creative balance between cast, crew, writers, execs, etcetera. That doesn't mean it was without conflict, it means the nature of that conflict, and what that conflict produced—the process—*that* was as close to a perfect experience as I think anyone deserves. Despite the show's credo, 'All this will happen again,' I just don't believe you get to live that way twice, not in one lifetime. That's why it's called science fiction."

Ron Moore is a bit more concise, but still equally gratified. "I'm so proud of it overall. It's just such an amazing thing to have been part of. I love the beginning. I love the end."

ABOVE: The "Nuclear Earth" ruin plans and concept design resulted in one of the bleakest images of the series. The Colonial Fleet finally discovers Earth in the episode "Revelations" only to learn that it does not hold the promise of salvation that they have been searching for.

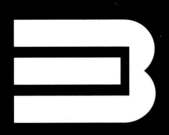 

CAPRICA

BATTLESTAR GALACTICA MAY HAVE ENDED when the Colonial fleet reached the planet they would name Earth, but the universe they'd existed in still had many stories to share. And while David Eick was correct that he wouldn't get to "live that way twice," the producers were not done with the franchise. Even though "Daybreak" had a definite finality to it—a couple of millennia worth of closure, to be sure—the franchise had more tales to tell through prequels and flashbacks that explored different facets of the story the audience thought they already knew.

A month after the final episode of *Battlestar Galactica* aired, the prequel series, *Caprica*, premiered on DVD and digital download. Set fifty-eight years before the fall, the series followed two families on the central planet of the colonies. From the planning stage, it was more of a family drama with soap opera elements than a space-faring adventure, setting itself apart from all of the *Battlestar Galactica* series that preceded it.

LEFT: Promotional images for *Caprica* centered on Zoe Graystone (Alessandra Torresani) both in her own body and as the Cylon model holding an apple. Allusions to the biblical Eve showcased Zoe's role in the franchise and the Colonials' history.

  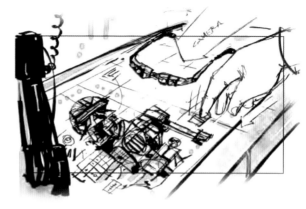

The first of these families was the Graystones, who were ultimately responsible for the birth of the Cylons and, in a roundabout way, the robots' introduction to monotheism. The other family that became inextricably tied to the Graystones was initially known by the name Adams. It was quickly revealed that their original surname—that they would later return to—was Adama. To play the patriarchs of these families, the producers went with established actors in Eric Stoltz, for the entirely new creation of Daniel Graystone, and Esai Morales, for the man audiences knew by reputation as Joseph Adama.

As Ron Moore notes, it was only natural to include a familiar family in the prequel, and the most logical choice would be the one tied to the male leads of *Battlestar Galactica*. "You kind of felt like if you're going to do a prequel, one of the very first questions you deal with is what are the ties to the beloved characters already? If we're going to go back in time and tell the prequel story, whose ancestors are we going to deal with? Because the audience is going to be looking around."

It had already been established that William Adama's father was a lawyer. This immediately made for a natural break from *Galactica* as Joseph Adama was in a different field than his son and grand-

sons. "He wasn't just another military commander, which would be just like Commander Adama," Moore says. "So already that's interesting." It became more interesting when the producers decided to make him a lawyer for the Tauran mafia, which would be a surprising revelation for an audience unaware of the family's darker side.

"I didn't want to do a lot of the rest of [the original characters]," Moore adds, explaining that the Adama family was the point at which the ancestral links to *Battlestar Galactica* would end. "I was like, 'Let's just do Adama—and maybe at some point down the line maybe we run into somebody else's grandparent—but he's going to be our one family tie to

the series.' But the show is really about the creation of the Cylons."

The edict to focus on the Cylons allowed the writers to fill in a lot of the backstory that had already been established, but never fully detailed. *Battlestar Galactica* delved into the history of the Cylons, but there was still a wealth of information to explore, revealing just how these creations of man had come to have sentience and strike out on their own, attacking their creators. Had *Caprica* lasted more than one season, there was a good chance one of the Final Five Cylons—Ellen and Saul Tigh, Samuel Anders, Tory Foster, or Galen Tyrol—would have appeared to provide an integral link between the two shows.

ABOVE: Storyboards for a television series are not only used to layout the scenes within an episode; they can also be used for other purposes. The above images are taken from the third pass on the storyboard for the *Caprica* title sequence which drew viewers into the world and its characters while credits rolled for the series.

IN THE BEGINNING...

Caprica began its development while *Battlestar Galactica* was still in its infancy. David Eick and Ron Moore had been toying with the idea of a spin-off while they were still exploring their new universe. But the needs of their production schedule made a second show a difficult proposition.

Around the same time, Remi Aubuchon, a writer on *24* and several other television series, pitched Syfy a TV series about the creation of an artificial intelligence that served as a science-fiction allegory for slavery. Seeing similarities between this and the concept that Eick and Moore had been considering, Syfy put the trio together to see if they could work something out. Eick, Moore, and Aubuchon merged the two concepts and *Caprica* was born.

By the start of the third season of *Battlestar Galactica,* the newly minted team was hard at work on the new concept with a pilot script already in development. But their work would remain in development with Syfy because the network wasn't yet willing to make a commitment to the series. It wasn't until the Writers' Strike during the 2007–08 television season that the idea finally became feasible, simply because it was one of the few scripts available.

The Writers' Strike lasted three months, but it shut down production on most television shows and on movies for a longer period. In the lead-up to the strike, studios held back on commissioning new projects since there was no point in starting production on a TV show or film only to have it shut down with a strike right after it got off the ground. When the strike was finally resolved, this led to fewer concepts in development when everyone was ready to get back to work. Conveniently for all involved, *Caprica* was ready to receive a green light.

Rather than a traditional series order or even a miniseries, *Caprica* launched with a DVD release of the pilot movie that also became available as a digital download. The story was divided

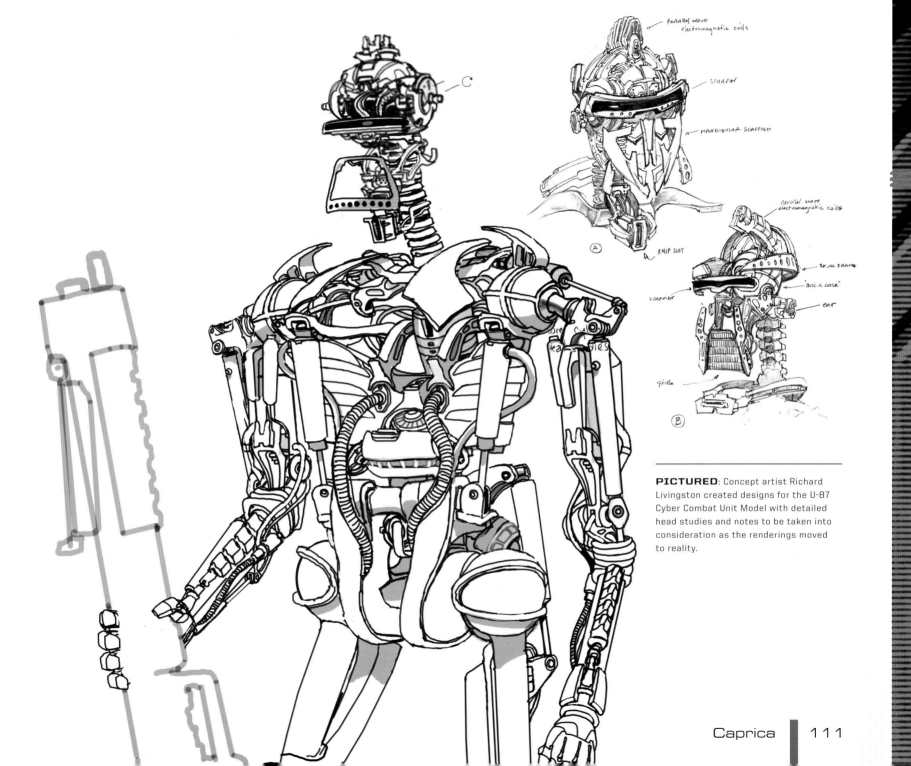

parallel wave
electromagnetic coils

scanner

MANDIBULAR SCAFFOLD

C

CHIP SLOT

A

parallel wave
electromagnetic coils

SKULL FRAME

scanner

"BRAIN CASE"

ear

grilla

B

PICTURED: Concept artist Richard
Livingston created designs for the U-87
Cyber Combat Unit Model with detailed
head studies and notes to be taken into
consideration as the renderings moved
to reality.

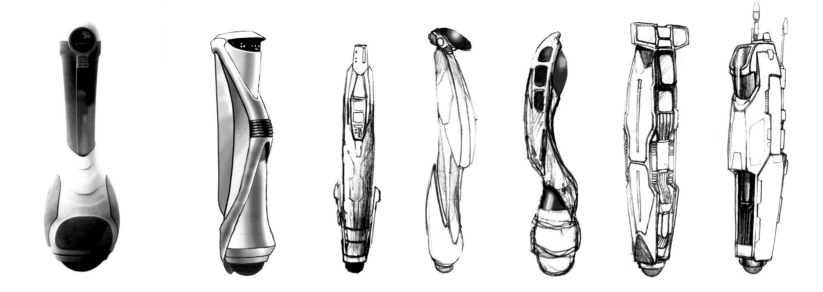

between the two families that would become inextricably linked through a tragedy motivated by religious zealots working under the auspices of the belief in the One True God. This would be the point in human history where, as seen in *Battlestar Galactica*, the shift in the Colonials' belief system from polytheism to monotheism would begin. This change would affect their robotic creations in ways that no one could have anticipated.

Caprica continued *Battlestar Galactica*'s exploration of religious themes, moving these stories to the forefront with the science-fiction elements ever-present, but fading into the background. From that initial pilot, the producers set up a world that was both familiar and unlike anything the audience had imagined. Caprican society was on the verge of a golden age of technology in which anything was possible. And yet, at the same time, the central world of the

ABOVE: Richard Livingston developed several different looks for the robot valet, Serge, providing a size comparison to humans as part of the development of the character.

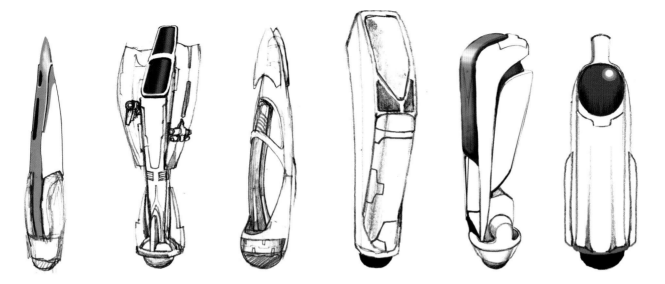

Colonies had a dark underbelly lived out in the Virtual World. Of course that golden age, as the audience already knew, was about to come to a crashing end with the First Cylon War.

A series order quickly followed the popular release of the original movie on DVD, but the new series would not air until nine months later on Syfy. During the break between *Caprica*'s pilot and the weekly series, another entry in the *Galactica* mythos was

released with *Battlestar Galactica: The Plan*, a TV-movie that was also first available on DVD. *The Plan* retold the story of the early episodes of *Battlestar Galactica* through repurposed existing scenes mixed with new material. The storyline paralleled the early days of the series, showing already familiar events but from the Cylons' perspective.

THE LOOK OF CAPRICA

Visually, *Caprica* melded a bit of the old and the new, taking what *Battlestar Galactica* had created and expanding on it. Viewers had the chance to see more of Caprica City, which was the seat of the Colonial government. The series continued to film in Vancouver as its predecessor had, using location shoots that evoked the same feel of the city in the earlier production. For instance, similarities could easily be seen between the Graystone lakeside home and Baltar's own residence on the water.

The production designers settled on four distinct visual tones for the series that could be found in the real-world settings of Caprica City and Little Tauron versus the holoband creations of the Virtual World and New Cap City. They approached each of these settings differently to visually reveal the changing world of Caprica as its perfect society experimented with a decadent underbelly. Caprica City was all cool colors and modern structures, while Little Tauron was a throwback, almost to the American 1940s or '50s on Earth, complete with sepia tones. The V-Club in the Virtual World exposed a darker side to the series with louder, more frenetic action contrasted at times with emptiness in unfinished rooms with no visible walls. New Cap City presented the most dramatic look of the four settings with its stylistic design, which twisted the real world into a setting right out of a noir film.

To create these diverse settings, the production often relied on computer-generated scenery in place of actual sets or locations. This is another way that the *Galactica* franchise was helping to change the nature of television production. *Caprica* relied heavily on green screen effects to extend the backgrounds or create entire environments. This was predominantly used in the Virtual World creation of New Cap City and something that is seen more and more on television in shows such as *Once Upon a Time*.

Visual effects supervisor Gary Hutzel had started talking with the producers about these virtual sets early in the days of *Battlestar*

Galactica, even though the technology wasn't yet at the point where it was a viable option. "You would do a lot of set extensions on *Battlestar*," Moore explains. "Most notably the hangar deck. If you ever saw the big, long shot of the hangar deck, that was always, obviously, a green screen. We did stuff like that fairly regularly. But not like we did in *Caprica*."

The cost of virtual sets was an issue on *Battlestar Galactica*, but that resolved itself over time as the technology advanced. "Every year these costs come down," says Moore. "The equipment gets simpler and easier and cheaper to use. The effects can be rendered faster. Things just keep getting better. By the time we got to *Caprica*, it was starting to get to the tipping point where you could use virtual sets more and do it on a production schedule and a production budget. It was starting to become, in some ways, cheaper than building it. But not always."

Virtual sets may have cost less to construct, but the increase to post-production time also had to be taken into account. Sometimes

PICTURED: The V-World was a decadent place where death only meant a temporary reboot. The club in the pilot was filmed at the same location as the Opera House in *Battlestar Galactica*, elements of which can be found in the V-Club virtual extension concept art by Doug MacLean.

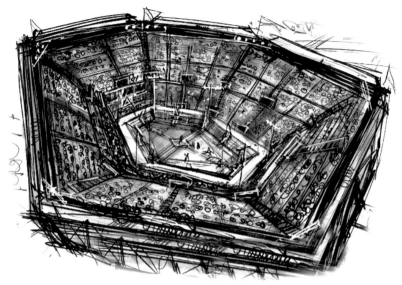

the trade-off meant that it was actually cheaper to build a set or rent a location. "All those shots have to be rendered," Moore explains. "Really, when you get down to the nitty-gritty of it and you really add up all the numbers, a lot of times [a virtual set] doesn't save you any money and it might end up costing you more. So, you still have to be wary of it. There's a temptation to just go to it because you think it's going to be cheaper, but a lot of times, it's not."

On *Caprica*, the producers looked at the scenes on a case-by-case basis, examining what they could afford to do and what met the needs of the schedule. "Sometimes it was a question of time," Moore adds. "If there's no time to build that set, we're definitely going to have to do it CG. Other times it's vice versa. It's like, 'Well, we can just knock off this on the soundstages for a tenth of the price it would cost them to do it if every shot is a visual effects shot. There was always this back-and-forth trade-off."

New Cap City contrasted the actual Caprica City almost like a photonegative. Where the actual city was bright and clean, the virtual one was dark and seedy, a natural evolution by the hackers that created it.

ABOVE: The game of Pyramid had a very different look in *Caprica* than the makeshift courts seen in *Galactica*. In the prequel series, the game was played in the giant, open-air stadium of Atlas Arena, which was a mix of practical set and VFX extension. The concept sketch on the left shows the layout of the physical set that would be merged with the CGI while the right image is a rendering of the VFX helicopter shot seen in episodes like "The Heavens Will Rise" and "Apotheosis."

The Virtual World and New Cap City became an immoral playground where death and seduction came easily as they had few repercussions in the real world of Caprica. Players of the holoband of every age could partake in their most base desires.

It was fitting that Sister Clarice's (Polly Walker) plan for apotheosis relied on stealing the technology that created this amoral playground and transforming it into the ultimate reward for believers of the One True God. In a series centered on teenage characters living in a world experiencing its own growing pains, *Caprica* explored deeper themes than the average family drama in much the same way its predecessor took a new approach to the space opera.

ABOVE: On the planet Gemenon a cathedral on a clifftop served as the headquarters of the Soldiers of the One as seen in the concept art for the green screen backdrop designed by production designer Richard Hudolin.

THE FALL OF CAPRICA

Like *Battlestar Galactica* before it, *Caprica* relied heavily on serialized storytelling. What began as a slow build took off throughout the season, ending in a race against time to stop Clarice's apotheosis. It was a race that fans were not sure they would have the chance to see all the way through.

Ratings for *Caprica* were not in line with *Battlestar Galactica*'s from the start and slowly dropped throughout the season. Once again, the audience was not necessarily watching the series as it aired on network, often preferring to see it through more convenient viewing methods. It didn't help when the freshman series was taken off the air for an unusually long mid-season hiatus, returning with even lower ratings than before.

Syfy announced the series' cancellation in October 2010 without airing the final four episodes. Those episodes were released a couple of months later on DVD and Syfy did eventually air them in a marathon viewing session that revealed one final gift to the fans.

ABOVE: In a piece entitled "Adama's community and outerlands" the concept art for the green screen designed by Richard Hudolin shows a bit of the Tauron community that is markedly different from the modern skyscapers of Caprica City.

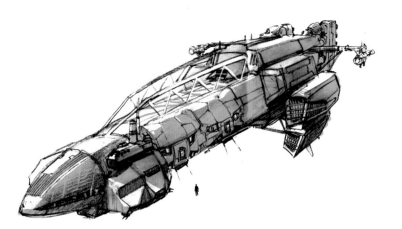

"That was our Hail Mary pass," Moore explains. "The network was not as supportive as they could have been that last season. The ratings were okay to mediocre, so in fairness to them, it wasn't like we were knocking it out of the park every week. But we wanted a little bit more faith given what we had done on *Galactica* ... As we got into the latter stages of season one it became clear that [network executives] were skeptical and we were starting to feel the writing on the wall that we probably weren't going to get a second season. We were just looking for ways of giving [the fans] something."

In Glen Larson's original *Battlestar Galactica*, each new hour of the show began with clips of the episode viewers were about to watch. This tease helped lure them in, though one could say that they were already there by simply turning on the television. This tradition was carried over in the reimagined version, with clips occurring in rapid-fire succession to the beat of the title theme, ending with the *Battlestar Galactica* seal. When it came time to air *Caprica*'s final episode, the producers expanded on this tradition by showing scenes from the upcoming second season that would never materialize. The scenes bridged the gap between the prequel and *Battlestar Galactica*, giving hints about the evolution of the hybrids, revealing why the Cylons found religion, and explaining how Willie Adama managed to die and still exist sixty years later.

"The network surprised me by letting me add that cliff-hanger, knowing that we didn't know our second season fate yet," Eick adds, noting that he did not share Moore's skepticism in a renewal. "The

ABOVE: Richard Livingston's concept art for planetary shuttles seen in *Caprica*.

truth is, I was so convinced the show would get a second season, we killed ourselves to nail that epilogue, worked harder on it than some entire episodes—conceiving the storyline, storyboarding every shot, being on set, reshoots, fine-cutting it ad infinitum over weeks and weeks, an elaborate sound and music design, micromanaging the shit out of the VFX. It's one of my favorite bits of the entire series and none of it mattered!"

The clips that would become an epilogue to the series required a delicate balance to show what was to come without giving too much away. "We were jumping ahead in our own story," Moore admits. "We were just grabbing things. 'Okay, let's show and do something that could be a promise of next year, both to the audience and to the network at the same time. And if this is, indeed, the last episode of *Caprica,* at least you'll have had an idea for where the story was supposed to go.'"

Once again, the end of a series did not necessarily mean the end of the *Galactica* universe. Two years after *Caprica* was taken off the air, a new entry into the mythology would premiere in another media format.

Battlestar Galactica: Blood and Chrome originated as a series of webisodes that together combined into one TV-movie released on DVD and for digital download. Another prequel to the reimaginged *Battlestar Galactica*, this story was set ten years into the Cylon War, following a young William Adama (Luke Pasqualino) on his first station aboard the *Galactica.*

There was talk of the movie becoming a backdoor pilot for another *Galactica* universe series, but it ultimately reverted to being a stand-alone episode in the history of the franchise. Considering that ever-expanding franchise began with a TV series cancelled after one season over thirty-five years ago, it may not be the last time a ship named *Galactica* flies through the cosmos in search of that shining planet known as Earth.

RIGHT: Zoe Graystone in the resurrection bath in her father's lab. This would be the "first" Cylon birthing tub, designed by Richard Hudolin and rendered by Ken Rabehl for the preview of what was yet to come.

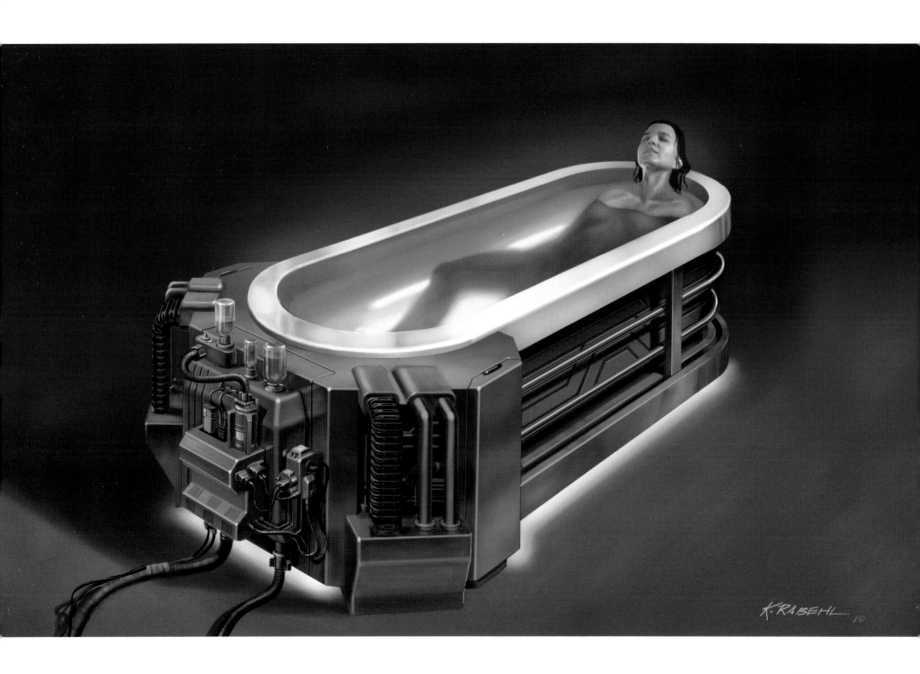

4 THE MYTHOLOGY OF THE TWELVE COLONIES

There are those who believe that life here began out there, far across the Universe with tribes of humans who may have been the forefathers of the Egyptians or the Toltecs or the Mayans ... that they may have been the architects of the Great Pyramids or the lost civilizations of Lemuria or Atlantis.

Some believe that there may yet be brothers of man who even now fight to survive, somewhere beyond the heavens!

LEFT: The story of the Colonial fleet began on a distant planet long before the Cylon attack. Kobol was the mother world of the Twelve Colonies. Its people were forced to flee in the fallout of a cataclysmic event. From the same planet, a mythical Thirteenth Tribe set out into space on its own.

THE TWELVE COLONIES OF MAN

On the surface, the original *Battlestar Galactica* seemed fairly basic in its premise: a society in ruin flees their enemy in search of a new home. To expand on that concept, Glen Larson and his team of writers hung the series on a human race that was as alien in language, customs, and references as it could be. They intentionally avoided the use of modern colloquialisms in dialogue that could place the series in the time period it was filmed. But what made *Battlestar Galactica* truly unique was the decision to make this human society alien in nature while at the same time tying them directly to Earth's history through a mythology that mirrored our own.

Glen Larson credits the book *Chariots of the Gods? Unsolved Mysteries of the Past* as providing inspiration for this idea. Written by Erich von Däniken in 1968, the book posits the following theory from the author: "I claim that our forefathers received visits from the universe in the remote past, even though I do not yet know who these extraterrestrial intelligences were or from which planet they came. I nevertheless proclaim that these 'strangers' annihilated part of mankind existing at the time and produced a new, perhaps the first, *homo sapiens*."

Larson found the idea of alien astronauts visiting Earth's ancient civilizations an interesting concept that bore further examination. What if the characters in his newly developing series were also related to these ancient astronauts? Or possibly they were the astronauts themselves?

With von Däniken's theory as a guidepost, Larson developed the mythology of the Twelve Colonies of Man, calling on allusions to a variety of human beliefs. This can be found in everything from the costume designs with obvious references to Egyptian culture to the very premise of the series that mirrored Moses's journey through the desert with the Israelites. Larson's own faith as a member of the Church of Jesus Christ of Latter Day Saints played heavily into the development of this new alien race as well.

Von Däniken's thesis is stated clearly in the prologue of "Saga of a Star World" and in several earlier episodes of the series, calling to mind the Egyptians, Toltecs, Mayans, and the like. It is also evident in the character names found in other mythology. Apollo is named for the Greek God of the Sun. Adama is the Hebrew word for Earth.

Of course, Larson's influences were not solely limited to mythology as Starbuck is a name most associated with the novel *Moby Dick*.

CHARIOTS OF THE GODS?

Unsolved mysteries of the past
ERICH VON DANIKEN

This moniker was presumably chosen for the fact that it contains the word "Star" as much as it was for any deeper meaning. Similarly, Apollo's name was originally intended to be Skyler, though it's possible it was both initially chosen and ultimately changed due to its similarities with the more familiar Skywalker.

In the mythology established by the original series, Colonial society originated on the planet Kobol. A disaster of indeterminate cause forced the people to "migrate to the stars" in search of new worlds to colonize. Twelve of those tribes settled on the worlds that would become the Colonies while a Thirteenth Tribe set out on its own path and found a new home on a planet they called Earth. Those

THIS PAGE: UK edition of *Chariots of the Gods?*, which was first published in Germany in 1968.

LEFT: Ralph McQuarrie's concept for the Cylon Basestar had a different look from the final version used on-screen, but the genesis of the circular ship can clearly be seen in the original sketch.

THIS PAGE: When the original series' script for "The Hand of God" called for scenes in the Cylon Basestar's hangar, a tabletop model was built with Cylon fighters parked on the deck. To enhance the perceived size of the miniatures, Universal Hartland used two scales of Cylon fighters. By arranging the two models carefully, the depth between them could be exaggerated and the miniature set made to look bigger than it actually was (above).

At right, the Basestar model being set up for a shot.

travelers mirrored the Twelve Tribes of Israel, descendants of the Jewish forefather, Jacob, who would follow Moses to the Promised Land.

As for humanity's point of origin, the name Kobol is an anagram of "Kolob," which translates to the "star closest to God" in the Mormon religion. The name can be found in the Book of Abraham, a publication Joseph Smith, founder of the Latter Day Saint movement, based on the translations of an ancient papyrus purportedly written by Abraham. In choosing that name for the planet, Larson again tied his story back to the Old Testament tale in which God told Abraham to go in search of that same Promised Land.

The all-powerful being—or beings—that the Colonials prayed to is where the religion of the series got a little murky. The Lords of Kobol are never fully defined in the original series, but it is stated that they were leaders on that home planet and possibly prophets. While several mentions of a single God are made in the series, the Lords of Kobol are spoken of with almost the same reverence. Of the

little information revealed about the Lords is that the Ninth Lord of Kobol was leader of the planet at the time of the exodus. His body is interred in the largest city on the planet, Eden, in a tomb that points to the location of Earth.

The planets of the Twelve Colonies took their names from the constellations of the zodiac, with Caprica (named for Capricorn) serving as the seat of the government. Like the Lords of Kobol, little is known about the planets of the Colonials in the original series. Some are not even named in the series or its sequel, *Galactica 1980*.

What *is* known is that each planet has a representative in The Quorum of Twelve (also known as The Council of Twelve) that leads the government of the colonies under the guidance of a president. Like the planet Kobol, The Quorum of Twelve also takes its name from the Mormon faith, though in a more direct fashion. The Quorum of the Twelve Apostles is the name for the ruling body of the Church of Jesus Christ of Latter Day Saints.

THIS PAGE: In "Saga of a Starworld," President Adar and The Quorum of Twelve gather on the *Atlantia* to celebrate the momentous occasion of the coming peace with the Cylons at the end of the Thousand Yahren War.

OPPOSITE PAGE: Ralph McQuarrie's art laid out not only the concept of The Quorum of Twelve, but ultimately could be seen as a storyboard for the opening scene of "Saga of a Star World."

FORGING A NEW PATH

"Saga of a Star World" opens on the eve of a peace conference between the Colonials and the Cylons at what was believed to be the conclusion of the Thousand Yahren War. (In classic *Galactica* vocabulary, a "yahren" is roughly the equivalent of an Earth year, though it does not necessarily equal the same time span. The average lifespan of a Colonial is two hundred yahren.) The beginnings of the conflict are vague, but it had something to do with the Colonials' involvement in aiding the Hasari in reclaiming their nation from the Cylons.

A member of The Quorum of Twelve, Lord Baltar had proposed the truce between the warring factions, but he was secretly working with the Cylons against his own people. Raiders attacked the peace conference as well as the other planets in the Colonies. A final confrontation occurred between the Colonial Fleet and the Cylons in the Battle

RIGHT: The Cylon attack on Caprica City (as seen through McQuarrie's art) was almost the end of the Twelve Colonies of Man. The sneak assault came on what was intended to be the signing of the peace treaty between the Colonials and Cylons. Serina and her son, Boxey, were among the few Colonials to survive the attack on the Caprica Presidium, but sadly, their daggit, Muffit, would perish in the conflagration.

of Cimtar, nearly wiping out the entire fleet save the lone *Battlestar Galactica* (and the later-revealed *Pegasus*).

The Colonials of the original series find Kobol rather quickly in their travels. The first two-part episode "The Lost Planet of the Gods" aired one week after "Saga of a Star World" in the US. The story begins with Apollo's announcement of his intention to wed Serina before the Viper pilots planning his bachelor party are stricken by an alien disease. Lacking available warriors, the fleet turns to

the crew training to be shuttle pilots, which is exclusively comprised of women, including Serina. What first appears to be a simple story about untrained pilots taking down a Cylon outpost shifts into something more dramatic when an area of space is discovered that matches a description in one of the Colonials' most revered texts.

In the Colonial religion, the Book of the Word is the cornerstone of their faith. The full depth of this book was never explored in the series as its single season only allowed for brief glimpses seen in

---

ABOVE: Stand-ins for the actors who played Adama, Serina, and Apollo approach the Pyramids at Giza when the production filmed in Egypt to recreate the discovery of the planet of humanity's birth, Kobol. It is in a tomb on the planet that Adama's medallion unlocks the planet's mysteries in a similar way to how the Arrow of Apollo acts as a key in the reimagined series.

computerized form. In "The Lost Planet of the Gods" it is stated that the book details the original exodus from Kobol that could potentially point the way to Earth.

"After their home planet Kobol was known to be doomed, the people set forth across a great void which seemed endless until a bright, shining star appeared as if from nowhere and guided them to safety."

The fleet discovers the planet Kobol by backtracking through that "great void." As with other elements of the series, the similarities with Earth's own history are obvious when a landing party reaches the planet and Adama, Apollo, and Serina set off to explore ruins that would be familiar to the audience. The production sent a small filming crew to Egypt to obtain shots of stand-ins for the actors approaching the Great Pyramids of Giza and exploring the temple at Karnak. The stand-ins are only seen from behind in the approach to the pyramids while the Temple is mostly viewed with an accompanying voice-over

from Adama. But those brief scenes clearly establish the Egyptian influences already seen in the warrior uniforms and other visual elements in the original series.

The medallion Adama wears matches the seal on the tomb. It is a symbol of power and faith, handed down through the millennia to each member of the Council of Twelve. When sunlight hits the medal at the proper angle, it becomes a key to open the tomb by reflecting light around the crypt. But a Cylon attack destroys the writings in the tomb that could lead to Earth and fatally strikes down Apollo's new wife, Serina.

Although a great deal of the Colonial mythology is explored in "The Lost Planet of the Gods," the Colonials—and the audience—end up with more questions than answers. Adama is even more intent on his search for Earth, but with their most promising lead destroyed, they are heading even more blindly into the stars with only their faith to guide them.

FREEDOM OF CHOICE

Almost a dozen episodes later, "War of the Gods, Parts 1 & 2" takes an important step in expanding the mythology of the series and delving into the religious beliefs of the Colonials. From a production standpoint, it diverges from the largely stand-alone "threat of the week" episodes that had marked the series up until then. "War of the Gods" takes a more serialized approach to the storytelling, which was a rarity in the original series.

Unlike the reimagined series which was highly serialized, Larson's *Galactica* had to build its mythology selectively, embedding the information in larger two-part episodes such as "The Lost Planet of the Gods" and "War of the Gods" rather than the traditional weekly installments. By making the contributions to the mythology more of an event, it likely helped ease network concerns that the viewers would fear missing important information. Later in the series, a four-episode arc led by the two-hour episode "Greetings From Earth" and culminating with "Experi-ment in Terra" would further expand on the mythology.

At the opening of "War of the Gods," a mysterious Ship of Light appears and abducts Viper pilots and their vessels. At the same time, the fleet encounters a strange being named Count Iblis on a planet with a wrecked ship of unknown origin. It is later revealed that these two new entities are linked as they hail from the same dimension, but are on different sides in the battle of good and evil. Though Iblis claims that he intends to lead the fleet to Earth if they appoint him their leader, it quickly becomes clear that he is on the side of evil. Commander Adama is the first to suspect Iblis's motives might not be pure, leading to an interesting exchange on the nature of God in the universe:

Iblis: I fear no man, no creature.

Adama: Not even God?

Iblis: What do you primitive children know of what you call God?

Adama: Only that we have been given laws which cannot be broken by any man or creature.

RIGHT: The Ship of Light (also known behind-the-scenes as the Lightship), was a vessel of incredibly advanced technology that made its first appearance in "War of the Gods, Part 1." The model for the ship was composed of neon light tubing and plastic fluorescent sheeting cut into strips.

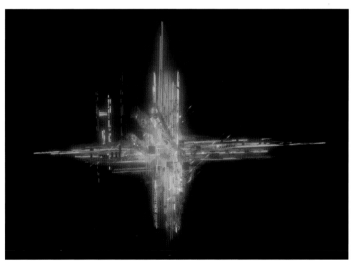

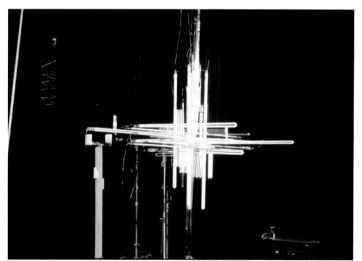

Iblis: Those laws do not apply to me.

Cylon history is also revealed when Baltar—who has turned himself over to the fleet—notes that the stranger has a voice similar to the Cylon Imperious Leader. Iblis explains that it is no coincidence. He is a member of the original race of Cylons that were taken over by their technology a thousand yahren ago. This suggests that Iblis is at least that old, which feeds into a theory Adama develops when he reveals to Apollo that he possesses mind tricks of his own that he has honed through intensive study. He essentially shares von Däniken's theory from *Chariots of the Gods?* that an advanced species would appear as Gods with the ability to do miraculous things to a race that was not as enlightened.

The Ship of Light that exists in a dimension "quite apart from [the fleet's] own" is populated by beings that the Colonial ancients called "Angels." They are custodians of the universe; highly advanced beings that are the "Light of Good and Truth, fighting the forces of darkness and evil throughout the stars." They have found kinship in the Colonials, claiming, "As you are now, we once were. As we are now, you may become." According to these beings, the Colonials are destined to evolve and to seed and nurture new civilizations. To help give them a start, they provide Apollo, Starbuck, and Sheba with important coordinates on their route to Earth, though they do not allow the trio to remember how they came about the information.

Earth Quadrant Alpha: Nineteen million sectars by Epsilon vector-22 on a circular reckoning course of 000.9, in a star system with nine planets and one sun.

Apollo and Starbuck will meet with these "Angels" or "Beings of Light" once again in "Experiment in Terra" when they find a planet they initially believe could be Earth. The episode comes at the end of a mini-arc in which the planet Terra is introduced (*Terra* being another name for Earth in the Gemenese tongue). Interestingly, the residents of Terra have names such as Michael, Sarah, Charlie, and Brenda, which are similar to names

THIS PAGE: The concept art of Count Iblis's introduction in "War of the Gods, Part 1" was drawn by artist Frank Frazetta, who would also create covers for some of the tie-in novels for the series. Iblis is revealed as a powerful being in the imagery, which carried through in the performance of the man who played him, Patrick Macnee. (Also in the photo: Anne Lockhart, Richard Hatch, and Dirk Benedict.)

found on Earth at the time the series aired, unlike the more historical names of the characters in the Colonial fleet. This could be an unspoken suggestion that they are descendants of the Thirteenth Tribe.

The planet Terra is on the verge of a nuclear holocaust, which is what brings the Beings of Light into the story. They require Apollo's help in averting the disaster since they cannot involve themselves directly due to their refusal to interfere with any person's freedom of choice. This concept was established in their introductory episode, "War of the Gods" when they used the same reasoning to explain why they did not stop Iblis from performing his evil acts.

The edict of noninterference prohibits the Beings of Light from averting a nuclear holocaust. They manage to work around it by placing Apollo into the body of a Terran named Charlie to have him come to the planet's aid. Interestingly, this episode seems to lay the groundwork for Donald Bellisario's future series *Quantum Leap* in which a man travels through time inhabiting people's bodies to help them "put right what once went wrong."

One could argue the point that the Beings of Light are interfering by injecting Apollo into Terra's conflict, but it raises interesting questions about the concepts of fate and personal freedom. If the Colonial fleet

ABOVE LEFT: Starbuck (Dirk Benedict) on the Ship of Light in "War of the Gods, Part 2."

ABOVE RIGHT: "John," who spoke for the Beings of Light, was played by Edward Mulhare, an actor who would go on to a more substantial role in Glen Larson's later series *Knight Rider*.

is destined to nurture new civilizations, how will that impact their relationship with the people of Earth? If they are the alien travelers from an advanced civilization, how will they approach the indigenous people of Earth if they are at an earlier stage of development?

In some ways, this concept is similar to the Prime Directive in *Star Trek,* which prohibits Starfleet officers from interfering with pre-warp societies. This rule grew partially out of the concern that less enlightened races might see the Federation as Gods due to their advanced technology, which is something of a common theme in science fiction along with von Däniken's influence.

ABOVE: Under the guidance of the Beings of Light, Apollo visits the planet Terra where he meets Brenda (Melody Anderson) and other residents who may be related to the sought-after Thirteenth Tribe.

THE SHINING PLANET

The final episode of the original series may be titled "The Hand of God," but it had no ties to the mythology of the Lords of Kobol or the Beings of Light. Instead it was an action-packed episode in which a message on an old, unused gamma frequency leads the fleet to a Cylon Basestar ripe for a surprise attack. Adama, perhaps with the memory of Commander Cain prompting him, decides to go on the offensive to deal a crippling blow to the Cylons.

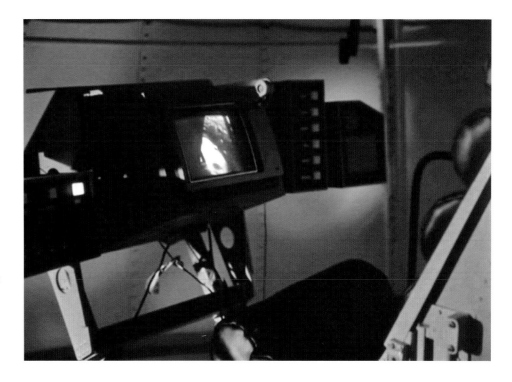

Aside from being the final episode of the original *Battlestar Galactica* and being popular among fans, "The Hand of God" is most notable because it contains the fleet's only true contact with Earth. At the very end of the episode, Apollo and Starbuck leave the celestial dome moments before a new transmission is received over gamma frequency: a video of the Apollo moon landing in 1969. The series fades out on the promise that Earth is real and the hope that some day the Colonial fleet may reach their new home.

This was also, according to Glen Larson, the result of one of the biggest battles he had with Donald Bellisario over the course of the series.

As he recounted in his interview for the Archive of American Television, Larson wanted to preserve the mystery of whether *Battlestar Galactica* was set in Earth's future, its past, or its current timeline. Unaware that this would be the final episode of the series when it was being filmed, Larson believed that by tying in the moon landing that occurred in 1969, it limited the direction he could take the story if the fleet ever did find Earth.

ABOVE: File footage from the Apollo moon landing in 1969 would be an integral piece of video in the series, confirming to the audience, at least, that Earth was real and possibly within reach.

Larson only relented when he became convinced that with the many unknown variables of the universe, a message from Earth could theoretically be bouncing around time as well as space. The scientific validity of such a belief is certainly up for debate, but it was that question viewers of the original series were left to wonder as the series ended on April 29, 1979.

Galactica 1980 would seem to answer the question definitively as the series took place on Earth. But Larson himself has largely dismissed that series, so it is difficult to say how it fits into the official canon of the show. The reimagined series that followed decades later, however, took up that question and most definitively answered it—in a way that would have made Erich von Däniken proud.

THE TWELVE COLONIES OF KOBOL

What the original series established in terms of mythology, David Eick and Ronald D. Moore built from and expanded for the reimagined *Battlestar Galactica*. The Twelve Colonies and Thirteenth Tribe returned, with their Lords of Kobol to worship and Cylon enemies to fight. The new *Galactica* would forge its own path through the stars, ultimately fulfilling the premise born from *Chariots of the Gods?* and the words of the Beings of Light as the Colonials evolved to seed and nurture a new civilization.

The world had become a different place in the decades between the two *Galactica* series. The seventies may have had their own turbulent times, but the television-viewing public of the new millennium witnessed more of the darkness in the world thanks, in part, to twenty-four hour news cycles. Fictional television series evolved beyond the need to neatly resolve storylines in an hour, while audiences became much more cognizant of a world in which problems weren't always wrapped up so cleanly.

The terrorist attack on the World Trade Center in New York on September 11, 2001 had a cultural impact on American television audiences

as well as the people who created their entertainment. "Escapist" television gave way to more thought-provoking fare. Television was never the "idiot box" some claimed it to be, but in the new millennium, TV writers were taking a more literary approach to their work, and the reimagined *Battlestar Galactica* was one of the shows leading that charge. One of the ways this presented itself in the new franchise was through the exploration of religious belief and zealotry in particular. What would happen when societies used their belief system to justify horrific acts of terror?

The shift in the Colonial belief system from a polytheistic society to one that followed a single God would be the backbone to *Bat-tlestar Galactica* and its prequel, *Caprica*. But the heart of this idea had come directly from the original series, inspiring Moore to take it in a new and interesting direction. As he explains, "The fact that this show had all these Greek God names for so many things: You had the Twelve Colonies, they were definitely astrological-based, or zodiacally-based. All the talk in the show was going to be referring to these things that had religious and mystical connotation to it. So, it was kind of an easy step to say that they're the pagans because they believe in multiple Gods and our enemies are the monotheists, reversing what we typically think of as the heroes and the villains

ABOVE, LEFT TO RIGHT: Banners of the Colonies: Caprica, Aquaria, Picon, Aerilon, Tauron, Gemenon, Canceron, Leonis, Virgon, Libran, Scorpia, and Sagittaron.

in our history of western civilization. I loved that. That was already interesting and fascinating."

Once again, Moore called on lingering frustrations from the time spent on his beloved *Star Trek* to inspire his later work. In particular, he still had issues with the long-running franchise's portrayal of religion, or lack thereof, in Earth's future. "It drove me crazy in *Star Trek*, it really did," he admits. "One of the things I just always objected to was this notion that in the future all of human society has just given up religion … All the main religions of the human race are gone in like three hundred years? I didn't believe it. I just thought that was fatuous.

ABOVE: Tomb of Athena concept art by Ken Rabehl, depicting the statue of Apollo where, once placed, the missing arrow would open a portal revealing the coordinates to Earth.

It's not going to just vanish. It might change. It might evolve. It might be a minority opinion instead of a majority opinion, but the Muslims, the Hindus, the Christians, and the Jews are not just going to go, 'You know what? This is all bullshit' in three hundred years. I always thought there was a falsity of *Star Trek* and I wanted *Galactica* and *Caprica* to say, 'Well, no. Actually human experience usually has [religion] as part of its reality, so let's make it part of their reality as well."

The Colonials and Cylons weren't simply presented as religious societies that held equal and opposing belief systems. The writers crafted each character to follow her or his own doctrine. Sister Clarice and Brother Cavil possessed strongly held convictions they relied on to twist their perception of what was right. Laura Roslin and Gaius Baltar found religion through their harrowing and mystical experiences. William and Lee Adama had a respect for religion, but did not seem particularly beholden to it. Moore felt it was important that there be different levels of belief among the Colonials and Cylons, with some even being atheistic, reflecting the makeup of our own society.

Moore did not have any specific message in his approach to writing *Battlestar Galactica* and *Caprica*. He was more interested in exploring themes of religion and allowing the audience to make their own judgments. "What I liked most conceptually was the opportunity to deal with the fact that religion is an important part of the human experience in our history of a people," he says. "For thousands of years, there is this recurrent theme of, 'We want to believe in something greater. We want to believe in something else.' We call it by different names and we've constructed different religions and different theologies around it, but the constant strain is that there is this need and desire to believe or to deny belief. There's this ongoing conversation about 'Who are we and why are we here?' I thought it was great that a science-fiction show could address that instead of pretending that in the future all that has vanished."

PICTURED: The Tomb of Athena developed from Ken Rabehl's initial sketches for the interior and entrance (left), through the cross-section plan that laid the groundwork for its creation (right) and finally to construction, painting, and set dressing to give it the look of ancient ruins (above).

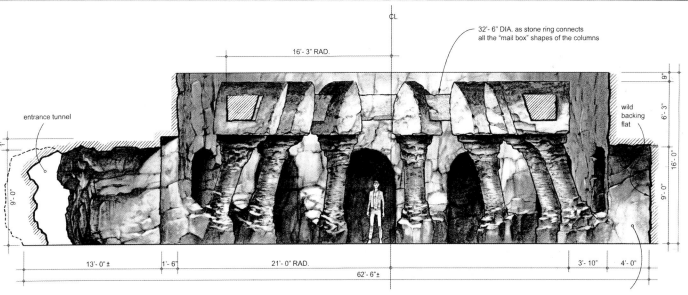

entrance tunnel

9'- 0"

1'

13'- 0" ±

1'- 6"

21'- 0" RAD.

62'- 6" ±

16'- 3" RAD.

CL

32'- 6" DIA. as stone ring connects all the "mail box" shapes of the columns

9"

6'- 3"

wild backing flat

16'- 0"

9'- 0"

3'- 10"

4'- 0"

ABOVE: The planet Kobol in the reimagined series was not as overtly tied to Earth as it was in the original series, but the ruins of The City of the Gods had definite roots in familiar architecture seen in the real world. Here, the set is being decorated to match the panoramic concept sketch of the ruins on Kobol designed by Richard Hudolin.

A BRIEF HISTORY OF TIME

In both the reimagined *Battlestar Galactica* and *Caprica,* religious zealotry is the basis for much of the action. The crux of the story is the conflict between this polytheistic society with a dozen Lords of Kobol and the opposing monotheistic belief in the One True God.

Mirroring the original *Battlestar Galactica*, the mythology for the new Eick and Moore franchise began on the planet Kobol, the origin point for all humanity. The first exodus from Kobol took place two thousand years prior to the events of the series, when the inhabitants were forced to abandon their home for reasons never fully explained in the series.

Prior to the exodus, humans lived on Kobol in peace with Lords who shared their names with the Gods of Greek mythology. The parallels with our own human history existed from the very origin of the Colonials' Gods, who also overthrew the Titans to take their reign. The residents of Kobol would pray to the Gods that befit their need, whether it be Zeus, the king of the Gods who lived on Mount Olympus, Athena, the Mother Goddess of Wisdom and War, or the others.

Like the original series, twelve of the tribes remained together during the exodus to establish new homes on the planets that would become the colonies, with names derived from the constellations in the Zodiac. A mysterious Thirteenth Tribe broke off from the others and went in search of a new home on their own, which became Earth. For much of history, the descendants from the planet Kobol believed that this last tribe was human, like themselves, but the Colonial Fleet would eventually come to learn that this was not true.

Thousands of years passed and the Colonials evolved into a more freethinking society. Some continued to carry on the traditions of their religion, while faith fell into the background for others. A select few began to question their Gods, including the sect that developed an idea of a One True God.

A new religion formed in the Monotheistic Church, under the lead-

ership of the Blessed Mother who believed in a single, all-powerful, omnipotent God. The movement reached its zenith fifty-eight years before the fall of the Colonies, at the same time as the construction of the first Cylons. These two events would become inextricably tied together, leading to the eventual fall of the Colonies.

The Soldiers of the One (STO), a militant arm of the religion, engaged in terrorist activities to spread their message. This is where the writers' visions took shape in the prequel series *Caprica,* exploring the idea of religious terrorism. Certainly, the Cylons decimating the Colonial race in *Battlestar Galactica* is the most overtly horrific act in the history of these

ABOVE: Sketch of the interior of the rock cathedral on Gemenon that was the headquarters for the Soldiers of the One as designed by Richard Hudolin.

people, but it is in the prequel series' human-on-human crime performed in the name of God that the message resonates almost more deeply.

Sister Clarice's (Polly Walker) vision for apotheosis relies entirely on the stolen holoband technology featuring the hack Zoe Graystone (Alessandra Torresani) developed to create a living avatar. In effect, the sister plans her own version of Heaven that true believers can enter upon death and live on forever in a perfect utopia. But it is not a true Heaven; it is another creation by man. In this case, by Zoe's father, Daniel Graystone (Eric Stoltz).

Almost from the start, the virtual world entered through the holoband had been conscripted for more base pursuits when the earliest licensors of the technology turned out to be adult entertainment companies. Hackers then took the initiative to delve into deeper forms of depravity by creating the V-Club and New Cap City. It is noble that Clarice wants to turn that dark place around to serve a higher purpose, if only her motives weren't so twisted.

These beliefs will translate into the ultimate destruction of the colonies through the Graystone family and the development of the earliest Cylons. When Zoe's program is downloaded into the very first Cylon model, it transfers through the duplicate copies, spreading the word of the One True God among the new creations. The message becomes more deeply ingrained when a number of models are illegally transported to Gemenon to serve the monotheistic church, coming into contact with Zoe's friend, Lacy (Magda Apanowicz).

Previews of the presumed "second season" of *Caprica* allowed the audience glimpses of the moments that would bridge the gap between *Caprica* and *Battlestar Galactica*. Daniel Graystone makes the first attempt at a hybrid Cylon, giving his daughter a second rebirth in the form of an android made to look human. This technology is not as advanced as the "skinjobs" that are seen in *Battlestar Galactica*, but it is a uniting point between the two societies, one that is exploited by "The Five" Cylons, and ultimately one that leads to the near end of humanity.

MODERN MYTH

Battlestar Galactica may have come before *Caprica* in production terms but it is set decades after the prequel and delves much more deeply into the ancient history of the colonies. At the same time, the impact of this new monotheistic belief system on the Cylons takes a commanding portion of the plot. *Battlestar Galactica* poses interesting questions about the nature of religion and the central theme of the series that "All of this has happened before and all of this will happen again."

This idea, known as the Eternal Return, can be found across multiple belief systems throughout human history. According to the Maha Yuga in the Hindu religion, Brahma destroys the universe and recreates it every 4.32 million years in an infinite loop. Called "The Cycle of Time" in the *Galactica* universe, its name and concept are similar to the Buddhist Wheel of Time. Western audiences are likely more familiar with Ecclesiastes 1:9, "What has been will be again, what has been done will be done again; there is nothing new under the sun." The core idea is that civilization will at some point end, but it will be renewed in a potentially endless cycle throughout history.

Laura Roslin (Mary McDonnell) shares the Colonial version of this idea in "Kobol's Last Gleaming, Part 1":

"If you believe in the Gods, then you believe in the Cycle of Time, that we are all playing our parts in a story that is told again and again and again throughout eternity."

The argument can be made that this core theme behind Eick and Moore's version of *Battlestar Galactica* almost stands in stark contrast to the philosophy laid out in Larson's original series. When writers of the original series established its mythology, they did touch on the concepts of fate and free will.

The mysterious Beings of Light functioned under the guiding principal that other beings should exercise their freedom of choice.

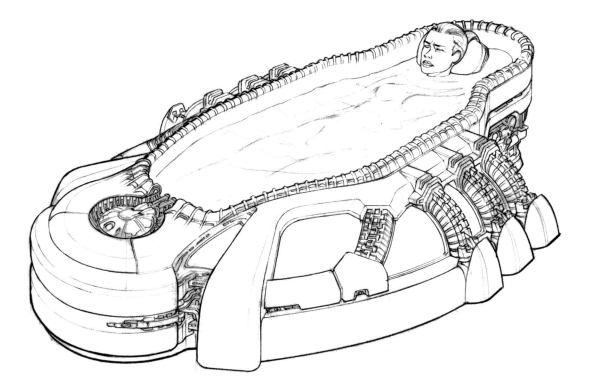

They refused to actively change the will of others, though they did manipulate forces in the direction they wanted things to move. Although there was no comment on whether it was a fruitless effort and humanity was destined to repeat its mistakes, it did imply that there was a purpose to this freedom of choice that negated the concept of fate. The reimagined series delved much more deeply into religion and philosophy than the original, taking this concept of destiny into the storyline as the Colonials made their second exodus from their homeland.

Resurrection is another theme explored in the franchise under Eick and Moore's guidance. In *Caprica*, Zoe Graystone and Tamara Adams (Genevieve Buechner) are reborn as avatars in a virtual space where

ABOVE: The rebirthing chamber sketch showcased just one of the ways the concept of death and rebirth was so important to the reimaged *Battlestar Galactica* and *Caprica*.

people can't truly die in most of the world. But the immortal decadence found in the V-Club gives way to New Cap City where avatars can experience "death." As a result, Zoe and Tamara's gift for returning to life elicits awe.

Battlestar Galactica incorporates resurrection directly into its story with the Cylons and their resurrection ship that makes them almost immortal. And in the end, Kara Thrace (Katee Sackoff) is born again as something other than human. But it is the opening miniseries that sees humanity reborn through a nuclear holocaust as the ultimate act of renewal.

The seeds for this action were laid in *Caprica* as an overreliance on technology, and the decadence of pursuits in the virtual world suggested that society had reached a point in which it was ready for this renewal. The fate of humanity is decided by the Cylons rather than any deity as they destroy their creators, setting in motion the events that will be played out in concordance with that which has occurred before. The fleet that survives is reborn in a new universe where people begin to question their faith and all they have known before.

Guiding the Colonials through this new awakening are the ancient Sacred Scrolls that detail the journey of the original exodus and project the path toward Earth. In the original series, Earth is almost a foresworn fact. There is no question that it exists to Lorne Greene's Adama. In the Edward James Olmos's reimaged version of this character, Earth is only a glimmer of hope, if not an outright lie. This changes slowly over the course of the series as Adama's confidant, President Laura Roslin, becomes more vested in the spiritual path she had never before embraced so deeply.

The Scrolls of Pythia will become the most important guidepost in the fleet's journey. These entries in the Sacred Scrolls were recorded 3,600 years earlier by the prophet Pythia. (In mythology, the Pythia is better known as the Oracle of Delphi.) "The Hand of God" episode

RIGHT: A visual effects version of landmarks resembling Earth's Stonehenge bears etchings that signify the Colonies and that are reminiscent of the symbols of the zodiac.

reveals that Roslin has been having prescient dreams, likely due to the chamalla extract she has relied on to manage her cancer. When she tells the priest, Elosha (Lorena Gale), she discovers that her most recent hallucination reads straight from one of Pythia's prophecies about a leader who suffers a wasting disease and would not live to enter the new land:

"And the Lords anointed a leader to guide the caravan of the heavens to their new homeland. And unto the leader they gave a vision of serpents numbering two and ten as a sign of things to come."

Like Moses being allowed to see the Promised Land, but forbidden to set foot inside, Roslin too was not intended to reach the fleet's ultimate destination. By the time the series reached its end, though, Moore felt like she had earned that right to set foot on Earth, so he changed her fate. Roslin would live to enter the new land, but she would die shortly thereafter, content in the knowledge that her followers had found salvation.

The discovery of the planet of humanity's origin in "Kobol's Last Gleaming" is an important step on that journey toward Earth. Their counterparts in the original series episode "Lost Planet of the Gods" may have come up empty when the tomb of the Ninth Lord of Kobol is destroyed, but these new Colonials found success in a map of the constellations surrounding Earth in Athena's tomb. The constellations, as is known from our own history, bear names similar to those of the Twelve Tribes that made up the colonies.

"When the Thirteenth Tribe landed on Earth they looked up to the heavens and they saw their twelve brothers."

The continuing journey to Earth is not an easy path. Much like the Israelites, the Colonials begin to question their destination. Like the Israelites' worship of a false idol, the battle between the old and the new religion is mirrored in the presidential election at the end of the second season. Incumbent President Laura Roslin wants to continue on the path their Gods had laid out while

her opponent Gaius Baltar (James Callis), with a little spiritual prompting, believes that the time has come to settle for a home beneath their feet.

The people choose a new path, but after a year of living in hardship, the relative peace on the planet comes to an end when the Cylons invade again. Though most of the Colonials eventually escape with their lives months later, Hera—the hybrid child of the human Karl Agathon (Tahmoh Penikett) and the Athena version of the Cylon Sharon Valerii (Grace Park)—is lost to the Cylons in the new exodus.

Hera is a pawn in the battle between the two religious doctrines from the moment of her conception. The first human-Cylon hybrid, she is a promise of hope to the Cylons, which makes her a potential threat to the fleet. The significance her role plays in history will not be revealed until the final moments of the series finale, but it is clear from the start that she will play a key part in the fate of humanity.

The Cylons have two objectives in the series—aside from the obliteration of the human race. They are looking to create life through procreation and they are searching for the parents who made them, the Five Cylons who adapted Colonial technology to give them life. In effect, they are searching for family.

In a vast departure from the intentions of the original series, it is revealed that the Thirteenth Tribe was made up of ancient humanoid Cylons, long predating the Centurion models created by Graystone Industries. This Tribe was also caught in the Eternal Return as Centurion models *they* built caused their destruction through a nuclear holocaust two thousand years earlier. The descendants of the Thirteenth Tribe all died in the apocalypse, save the Five Cylons that had rediscovered resurrection technology and created alternate versions of themselves that could live on after death.

These five remaining Cylons made their own journey to rediscover the Twelve Tribes, traveling thousands of years to warn of the potential danger of creating life through technological means. They arrived at a time when the Colonials were already at war with the Centurions. As a trade-off for calling a cease-fire, these Five Cylons—or *ancient astronauts*—would introduce advanced technology to the less enlightened Centurion soldiers to seed new life in the form of humanoid Cylons. But their first creation, Cavil (Dean Stockwell), turned against them, wiping their memories and setting them on new paths before bringing his brothers and sisters together in his plan to end the human race.

The Cylons commit horrific acts in the name of their religion and their quest to punish humanity for the treatment of their Centurion brothers. At the same time, they enslave the very Centurions they claim to be saving. They, too, are as lost as the fleet of Colonials, though they have diverged from a *spiritual* path. It takes a sect of Cylons, seeking their own form of forgiveness, to unite with the Colonials and find the ultimate reward in the continuation of their race and a chance to begin anew without the need for resurrection.

RIGHT: Costume design for Cylon Final Five by Terry Pitts.

Final Five
Battlestar Galactica
season 3 episode 10/11
Costume Designer Glenne Campbell

JOURNEY'S END.

Music played a central role in the reimagined *Battlestar Galactica*. It set the mood to the scenes and ultimately served as an important plot device on more than one occasion. Throughout the series, Composer Bear McCreary incorporated diverse musical influences from all over the world, leading up to the single most important composition used in the show, Bob Dylan's "All Along the Watchtower." That song would be a clue to the identity of four of the Final Five Cylons and it would point the way toward a new home for the fleet.

"All Along the Watchtower," originally released in 1967, may have seemed out of place in the alien fleet, but it was not the first time familiar references made their way into the show. Aside from the obvious allusions to Earth's history in the characters' names and Colonial mythology, more modern words and phrases slipped into the scripts. *Cloud Nine*, a name for one of the ships in the fleet, was taken from a popular phrase used in the twentieth century. At one point,

the capable yet morally circumspect Colonial fleet attorney, Romo Lampkin (Mark Sheppard), makes a reference to Wynken and Blyken, characters from a nineteenth-century poem entitled "Wynken, Blynken, and Nod."

When Glen Larson created the original *Battlestar Galactica*, he worked diligently to create a truly alien environment. While his show gave birth to those historical allusions to Earth, he and the writers also tried to avoid any modern colloquialisms, or anything really that took place *Anno Domini*. The Colonials had their own customs and a language that was just outside of the audience's own terminology; it was understandable while still noticeably foreign.

The reimagined series carried on that tradition, but also ignored it when the need served the storyline. As homage to the original series, the writers reintroduced "frak," a derivative of "frack," as an expletive and included the games of Pyramid and Triad (although Moore has admitted to getting the two confused, accidentally switching the names of the sport and the card game), but they also created their own language.

Again, Colonial terminology would be close enough to terms found in the English language that it could be easily understood by the viewing audience: *morpha* was used as a derivative of morphine, and the fleet's radio communication system was known as the *wireless*. They also relied on familiar words such as cancer, a disease the audience would immediately understand and react to. The similarities in language, history, and musical influence could easily be explained away by the final episode in which the audience learns that all this has indeed happened before and will happen again.

When musical notes taken from "All Along the Watchtower" lead Starbuck to the coordinates for "Earth," she fulfills her destiny as the one to lead the fleet to salvation and destruction. The fleet is saved in that they have found a home where they can finally end their journey. But it is also destroyed by the decision to eschew technology and spread out across the planet, sending the ships of the fleet into the sun.

Just as Roslin does not survive long beyond the discovery of Earth, Kara also sees her destiny through but then disappears, leaving the audience to wonder exactly what she has become.

In the final moments of the last episode, the audience learns that we "earthlings" are all descendants of the intermingled Colonials and humanoid Cylons. These ancient astronauts turned away from their technology so as not to impose themselves too greatly on the indigenous life on the planet. Without that technology they may not have appeared as Gods, but it is clear that their history and beliefs influenced the native beings. And Hera, who became mitochondrial Eve, founded an entirely new race of homo sapiens that continued to evolve for thousands of years.

The final montage of the series culls together clips of robotic creatures that already exist today, suggesting that humanity is still doomed to the Eternal Return as we work to recreate life in our own image.

Baltar: Man and Manifesto

Gaius Baltar is one of the more fascinating characters to appear on television in the new millennium. He was created in a decade that saw the antihero moving from a supporting character to the lead in darker series such as *Dexter, The Sopranos,* and *Breaking Bad.* As part of the ensemble of *Battlestar Galactica,* his personal journey in accepting God takes him from the darkest depths of his culpability in the near annihilation of the race of man to salvation in a new homeland, light-years from the sins of his past.

As a character, Baltar is more reactive than active. He rarely provides the inciting incident of the story, but his actions impact many of the characters in the fleet and the Cylons as well. He tends to make decisions in response to situations, rather than instigating them due to his conflicting nature as a strong personality with a host of weaknesses that allow him to be easily guided by others.

Baltar is the first of the characters visited by the messengers of a higher power that remains unnamed. In the Cylon faith, that being is considered a singular God, though it is later revealed the entity does not care for that moniker. The entity's messenger arrives in the form of the character that became known as "Head Six," who was representative of the Cylon that Baltar became involved with on Caprica that used him to

enact the planet's destruction. At first, it is unclear if she is a manifestation of Baltar's imagination or part of a Cylon plot, but as time passes, it becomes clear that she serves a higher purpose. She walks with Baltar every step of the way, just as a messenger in the form of Baltar will eventually attach himself to Caprica Six.

Every selfish act on Baltar's part results in a decision that brings him closer to salvation in accepting the "One True God." While his motivations are not usually pure, they are genuine and his actions are rewarded. But they very clearly do not follow any edict giving him freedom of choice. It is clear from the start that when he turns his back on God, he is punished, and when he accepts God, he is rewarded. At least until the point he rages against God, creating his own manifesto and inspiring followers of his own.

In the end, Baltar may not be redeemed, but he is forgiven. This absolution comes both at the hands of the Colonials, but also from whatever force in the universe is guiding things. He is last seen heading off with Caprica Six to live in peace, a farmer like his father before him, enjoying his days no longer in a struggle between Cylons and Colonials, presumably content with the belief system he has chosen for himself.

THIS PAGE: Concept art for Baltar's shrine, a key component in the evolution of the character in terms of his role in accepting the monotheistic beliefs of the Cylons and passing them on to his Colonial followers.

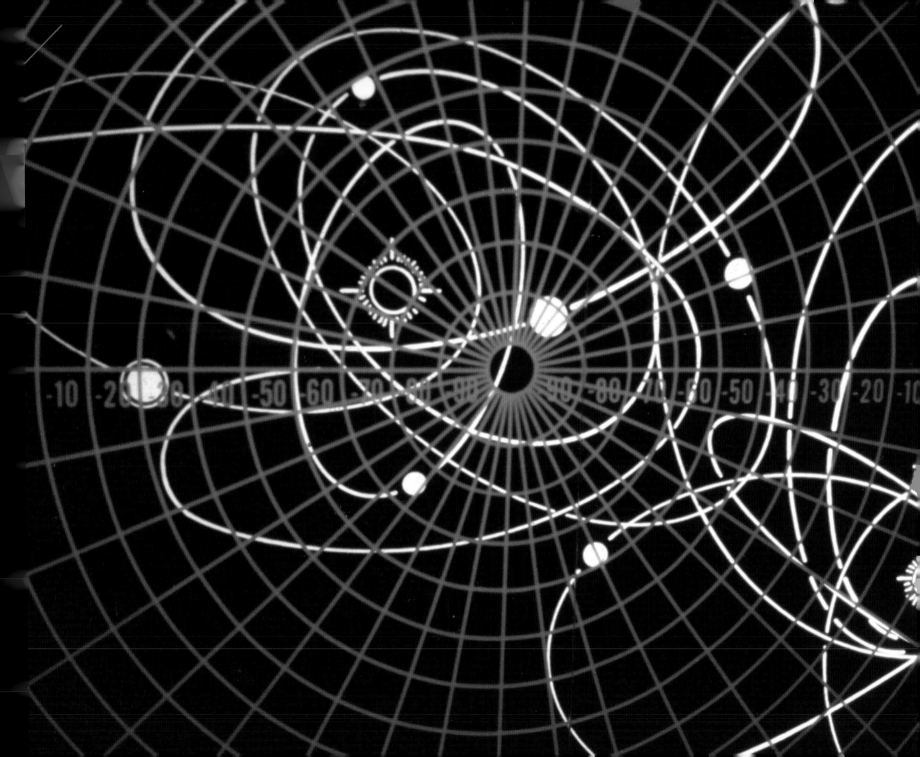

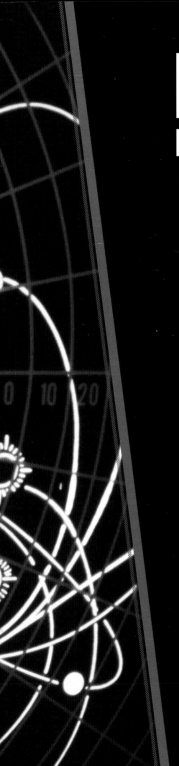

5 LEGACY

BY YOUR COMMAND

THE ORIGINAL *BATTLESTAR GALACTICA*'S LEGACY has lived well beyond those twenty-four episodes. It inspired a franchise that has lasted for over thirty-five years.

The hardcore fans who loved the show from its inception may know the series inside and out, but even casual viewers remember pieces of it for years to come. The catchy earwig of a theme song composed by Stu Phillips and Glen A. Larson is one element that has stood the test of time. The opening horns swelling in the *Battlestar Galactica* theme are instantly recognizable.

Phillips worked in the Universal Studios music department and was a longtime collaborator with Glen Larson. He created memorable scores for most of Larson's series, including *Knight Rider*, another popular theme. For many, the stirring music performed by the Los Angeles Philharmonic Orchestra would be an aural time machine, immediately transporting them to their youth. The tune even had a cameo in *Airplane II: The Sequel*. The familiar theme song was so deeply connected with the original series that the producers of the reimagined series decided to divorce themselves from it almost completely, using it sparingly, almost negligibly, in the series.

LEFT: The *Battlestar Galactica* universe began as a single season of a television series before expanding decades into the future with spin-offs, reboots, TV-movies, publishing, licensing, and a fan community that refused to let it end. This map charts the Exodus of the 13 colonies from Kobol.

When David Eick and Ron Moore approached the theme for the reimagined version, they had composer Richard Gibbs go in a completely different direction from the original. "I reflect on [the reimagined] *Battlestar Galactica*'s musical score as answering the call to subvert *Star Trek, Star Wars*, and all its subgenre descendants, including the old *Battlestar*," explains Eick. "That sparse, masculine, Asian-influenced, Taiko drum–centric score that Richard Gibbs designed, composed, and recorded (with director Michael Rymer's heavy influence, passing out on Richard's floor after combustible all-night composing marathons like something out of *Amadeus*) … was about as far from that standard-issue, fat, orchestral space opera bombast as it was possible to get. Respectfully speaking, the use of the original *Battlestar* theme in the pilot was, frankly, just sort of an inside joke."

When the original theme appears in the miniseries, it is during the decommissioning ceremony for the *Galactica*. In a way, it

---

RIGHT: Stu Philips's original handwritten music score of "The *Battlestar Galactica* Theme."

BATTLESTAR GALACTICA
PASSACAGLIA

composed and orchestrated by Bear McCreary

©2005 NBC Universal Television LLC
Published by Sci Fi Channel Publishing LLC, ASCAP
Intended solely for private or educational performance only

implies that the song is representative of the original series being decommissioned to usher in the new *Battlestar Galactica* and all the promise it held. But, just like elements from the original series that would pop up in the episodes that followed, the familiar theme song was not gone for good. Bear McCreary would call back to it again when he took over as composer for the weekly series, using it in D'Anna Biers's (Lucy Lawless) documentary on the *Galactica* crew when she was still in the fleet under the guise of a reporter.

Beyond that minimal use of the original theme, McCreary took the sound that Gibbs created in new directions. As the popularity of the show grew, McCreary presented concerts of his score, once bringing out Katee Sackhoff as a special guest to duet with him on the piano as her character does with her father in the episode "Someone to Watch Over Me." It was one of the many ways that fans were able to directly interact with *Battlestar Galactica*.

PREVIOUS PAGE: Original series composer Stu Philips conducting a recording session with the studio orchestra (left) juxtaposed with reimagined series composer Bear McCreary at the piano with James Callis (right).

LEFT: Bear McCreary's sheet music "Passacaglia," from the score for the episode "Kobol's Last Gleaming, Part 1."

SO SAY WE ALL

Communication with the fans of the reimagined *Battlestar Galactica* developed in interesting ways as the shape of television changed in the new millennium. But Eick and Moore certainly did not pioneer the idea of fan interactions.

Genre television shows—and science-fiction series in particular—have always inspired a devout fan base and the original *Battlestar Galactica* was no different. Universal Studios' intense media campaign included the traditional news outlets while also appealing to a younger audience by putting Starbuck (Dirk Benedict) and Apollo (Richard Hatch) on the cover of *Teen Beat Magazine,* among other publications. A strong licensing program, bolstered by the success of other popular genre properties, saw the characters and ships on everything from T-shirts to lunch boxes and board games. Books and comics continued long beyond

ABOVE: Katee Sackhoff and Bear McCreary perform "Someone to Watch Over Me." Photos by Andrew Craig.

the life of the series, including a novel series cowritten by Richard Hatch when he was trying to make the case for his own vision of a new *Battlestar Galactica* television series.

It was a fan campaign, encouraged by Glen Larson and the production team, which assisted in getting *Battlestar* back on the air after its cancellation. *Galactica 1980* may not have been the series the fans were expecting, but it was a seminal moment in television. Successful fan campaigns that send Tabasco sauce or nuts or demand six seasons and a movie from studios are almost commonplace today, but they were very rare back when *Galactica* was on the air. Even *Star Trek*—animated series notwithstanding—took almost a decade to return in live-action form.

The original *Battlestar Galactica* may have lasted for only one season, but it inspired a devotion in its fan base that stayed with the series for years. Fans even developed their own ways of socializing outside of the show that occurred long before the Internet became a playground for the masses. Hatch, in particular, was integral in keeping the show alive through fan involvement. In addition to the books and TV-show pitch he created, Hatch is credited with the idea for the first fan convention in 1993.

No stranger to devout fandoms, Moore was interested in exploring new online outlets for fan interactions when the reimagined series came along. So when the studio approached him about doing episodic audio commentary for the series, he jumped at the chance … once he learned what it was they were talking about. "At that point, I'd never heard the word 'podcast,'" he recalls. "I didn't know what it was. That was a whole new idea and I liked it. I thought it was cool because I liked doing DVD commentary tracks, but unlike having to go to a studio and sit in a room and block out a big chunk of time to go do a commentary track, they just gave me a tape recorder and I could just take it home and do it. That was the biggest advantage. I could do it whenever I felt like it at my house. It was very informal, so that's why I really gravitated toward it."

Moore's podcasts for *Battlestar Galactica* provided writers' commentary for the episodes in the final season and joined in an already active online presence. Moore takes the craft of writing seriously, and though he is not above making light of his own work, his podcasts, DVD commentary, and online Q&A sessions gave the fans a rare look at the process it took to bring their favorite show to the screen. Eick was part of that social media revolution as well, but he took a somewhat different approach.

Knowing that Moore wanted to do the audio podcasts, Eick decided to go in a related but alternate direction. "At that time,"

ABOVE: *Many Battlestar Galactica fans started young, like those at a special youth screening at the Plitt Century Plaza Theatre in Los Angeles, California on September 19, 1978.*

Eick recalls, "Peter Jackson was introducing something online no one had done before, which he called video blogs—little interstitials from the New Zealand set of his adaptation of *King Kong*. He hosted them himself, taking viewers on somewhat irreverent tours of the stages, introducing the actors, revealing secrets, playing pranks, making light of the whole thing. You saw him brushing his teeth in the morning, driving to work, struggling with the humdrum banality of moviemaking in an absurdist way that stripped it—and himself—of its untouchable mystery. I loved it. And, being the ham that I am, I ripped it off. And those became the *Battlestar Galactica* Video Blogs."

Their show would inspire its own devoted fan base of viewers who shared love, hate, and everything-in-between for what they saw on-screen. The advent of social media gave the fans new outlets to let their voices be heard, to bond and argue, and to even affect the very world they lived in.

FRAK

The franchise that is *Battlestar Galactica* has left an ongoing legacy for its creative and technical endeavors, but its most lasting contribution to popular culture might just be an expletive.

When Glen Larson created *Battlestar Galactica*, he developed a unique language for the Colonials. It was like our own in many ways and yet different enough that the audience could clearly understand the dialogue but appreciate that it wasn't what they were accustomed to hearing. As a part of that, he created a series of expletives the Colonials could use, which, being made-up words, would conveniently be approved by network censors. Of these words, two stood out at the time: frack (a stand-in for the "f" word we are accustomed to) and felgercarb (an alternate to "crap," which, in the reimagined series, became the brand name of the last tube of toothpaste in the entire fleet, after the destruction of the colonies). The show used these words sparingly and, aside from the more hardcore fans, they largely disappeared from public consciousness with the end of the series.

Decades later, Moore found inspiration in the word "frack"—though he changed the spelling to "frak" to make it a "four-letter word"—and incorporated it into the reimagined series. "Because they had done it on ABC television in the seventies, there was no way they were going to tell me I couldn't do it today," Moore states. "I just ran with it. They never used it in the way we used it: 'mother-frakker' and 'frak me' and 'frak this.' We really used it aggressively. It just made it a lot better and it made it more real and let the characters be themselves."

The word caught on with fans outside the series and lived on beyond the show's end. At first, online users would cite it in camaraderie, like a shared secret between those in the know. The word quickly took off, bolstered by usage on TV shows, such as *Veronica Mars*. Eventually, it would be seen on T-shirts and other licensed products. Even after the last installment of the franchise aired, "frak" had entered the popular lexicon, becoming an almost acceptable curse.

The *Battlestar Galactica* franchise has been groundbreaking in so many ways, from its use of visual effects on television to the ways the production team interacted with the fans through social media and at conventions. The stories of the various series in the franchise carried on the proud tradition of having science-fiction allegory comment on real-world issues of the time. It has been both escapist and inspiring in ways that have touched fans for decades. And it has even added a word to the language. What critics once dismissed as a clone of another franchise has grown and flourished to become its own entity that, to this day, continues to be praised and lambasted by anyone with an Internet connection.

IMAGE CREDITS

Page 127: Courtesy NBCU Archives & Collections (right).

Pages 129–131: Courtesy NBCU Archives & Collections.

Page 135: Courtesy private collection via Gene Kozicki (all).

Page 137: Courtesy Heritage Auctions (right).

Pages 144–147: Courtesy Gary Hutzel and Mike Gibson.

Pages 148–150: Courtesy Doug McLean.

Pages 153: Courtesy Gary Hutzel and Mike Gibson.

Pages 154–155: Courtesy Gary Hutzel and Mike Gibson.

Page 157: Courtesy Terry Pitts and Glenne Campbell.

Page 161: Courtesy Doug McLean.

Page 164: Courtesy Stu Phillips.

Page 165: Courtesy NBCU Archives & Collections (both left).

Page 165: Courtesy Bear McCreary (both right).

Page 166: Courtesy Bear McCreary.

Page 167: Courtesy Bear McCreary and Andrew Craig.

Page 169: © ABC Photo Archives/ABC via Getty Images.

Page 173: Courtesy Jerry Hultsch.

Removables:

Book of Pythia: Courtesy NBCU Archives & Collections (all).

Starbuck navigation art: Courtesy NBCU Archives & Collections.

Cylon poster: Courtesy Andrew Probert, Eric Chu, and Richard Livingston.

Storyboards: Courtesy NBCU Archives & Collections and Gene Kozicki.

Script pages: Courtesy Propstore.

Ralph McQuarrie poster for "Saga of a Star World": Courtesy John Scoleri and Stan Stice, RalphMcQuarrie.com.

1978 fleet: Original miniatures from the private collection of Gary Cannavo, photographed by E. Jim Small.

Malfunction memo: Battlestar Galactica: Season 1, Universal Studios Home Entertainment, 2005.

Behind-the-scenes contact sheet: Courtesy of NBCUniversal Archives & Collections.

THIS PAGE: Jerry Hultsch, Eick's friend from high school, created the animated R&D logos for the end of each episode. He wrote the skits and captured the photography, sound effects, and music. Before expanding his studio, Hultsch performed all of the voices for the animations during the first three seasons.

SOURCES

Documentary and Commentary

Archive of American Television interview with Glen A. Larson, conducted by Lee Goldberg, February 5, 2009

Caprica: Season 1.5, Universal Studios Home Entertainment, 2010

Caprica: Season 1.0, Universal Studios Home Entertainment, 2010

Battlestar Galactica: Season 4.5, Universal Studios Home Entertainment, 2009

Battlestar Galactica: Season 4.0, Universal Studios Home Entertainment, 2009

Battlestar Galactica: Season 3.0, Universal Studios Home Entertainment, 2008

Battlestar Galactica: Season 2.5, Universal Studios Home Entertainment, 2006

Battlestar Galactica: Season 2.0, Universal Studios Home Entertainment, 2005

Battlestar Galactica: Season 1.0, Universal Studios Home Entertainment, 2005

Battlestar Galactica: The Lowdown (and commentary), *Battlestar Galactica: The Miniseries*,
Universal Studios Home Entertainment, 2004

Books

Confessions of a Kamikaze Cowboy, Dirk Benedict, Square One Publishers, 2005

Chariots of the Gods? Unsolved Mysteries of the Past, Erich von Däniken, Putnam, 1968

Articles

"Fifteen Years of Galactic Battles with *Battlestar Galactica*," William E. Anchors Jr., *Galactic Sci-Fi
Television Series Revisited*, Alpha Control Press, 1995

"Fighting Hostile Rays, Evil Aliens—and Complex Lawsuits …," Bill O'Hallaren, *TV Guide,* September 16-22, 1978

"Fall TV Preview—Son of Star Wars: TV's *Battlestar Galactica*," *Newsweek*, September 11,1978

Author Interviews

David Eick (January 2014)

Ronald D. Moore (January 2014)

Gary Hutzel (April 2014)

ACKNOWLEDGMENTS

My deepest gratitude goes out to David Eick and Ronald D. Moore for their invaluable contributions to this book, along with additional thanks to Maril Davis, Jess Haber, Ben McGinnis, and David and Lili Rossi (and Frankie and Dash, too). Special thanks to everyone at becker&mayer!, Sterling Publishing, and NBCUniversal, with an extra-special shout out to Ben Grossblatt, Leah Jenness, Chris Lucero, Melissa Rauch, Jessica Nubel, Ed Prince, Kim Niemi, Dana Youlin, Nicole Burns Ascue, Emily Zach, and Sam Dawson. And finally, much appreciation to Matt Speer, Adam Sullivan, Ashley Gaetzman, Chris Miller, Keith Relyea, Ryan Neill, and the entire Valley Plaza crew, without whose generous support this book would have been impossible to write.

Thank you to Gene Kozicki for research assistance and fact-checking, and to Gary Hutzel, Mike Gibson, Katee Sackhoff, Richard Hatch, Doug McLean, Eric Chu, Richard Livingston, Terry Pitts, Bear McCreary, Dale Long, Brooks Peck, John Scoleri and Stan Stice of RalphMcQuarrie.com, Andrew Probert, Stu Phillips, Brandon Alinger, Jack Morrissey, and to Deidre Theiman at the NBCUniversal Archives & Collections.

Special thanks to Gary Cannavo for allowing us access to his prolific collection of original VFX miniatures, to photographer E. Jim Small (visit Small Art Works online at www.smallartworks.ca), and to Charles Adams, George Takacs, Daniel Umbro, and Phil Curl for assisting with model preparation.

ABOUT THE AUTHOR

Paul Ruditis is a *New York Times* best-selling author who has written or contributed to dozens of media tie-in novels, companion guides, graphic novels, and novelty books for TV shows such as *The Walking Dead, Bones, Charmed, Buffy the Vampire Slayer, The West Wing,* and *Star Trek.*

Published in 2014 by Aurum Press Ltd
74–77 White Lion Street
London N1 9PF
www.aurumpress.co.uk

Produced by becker&mayer! LLC, Bellevue, Washington.
www.beckermayer.com

A catalogue record for this book is available from the British Library.

ISBN: 978-1-78131-335-0

Design by Sam Dawson
Editorial by Dana Youlin and Nicole Burns Ascue
Photo Research by Emily Zach
Production Coordination by Tom Miller

Printed and bound in China

10 9 8 7 6 5 4 3 2 1
2018 2017 2016 2015 2014